LEAD

HOW EFFECTIVE
LEADERS GET
THINGS DONE

Gerald H. Graham, Ph.D.

Permission Information

These ideas first appeared as columns in the Wichita Business Journal and have been reprinted with permission.

Books Authored by Dr. Gerald Graham

Business: The Process of Enterprise
The World of Business
Management: The Individual, the Organization, the Process
Understanding Human Relations

Lead – How Effective Leaders Get Things Done

Cover design, book design and layout by Jim L. Friesen
Cover photo: Jim Meyers
Back cover photo: Paula Seiwert

ISBN-13: 978-0-9860184-0-4
ISBN-10: 0-9860184-0-6

Library of Congress Control Number: 2012947124

Printed in the United States of America by Mennonite Press, Inc., Newton, KS, www.mennonitepress.com

Dedication

I dedicate this book to my wife, Carol, a proven and encouraging leader; and to future leaders: Caroline, Dalton, Eliza, and Graham.

I also dedicate this book to the more than 750,000 managers and supervisors who have attended my leadership workshops over the past 45 years. These participants, with their years of experience and earned insights, allowed me to evolve, shape, refine and test my theories and practices against real-world leaders who were on the firing line every day.

Acknowledgements

I have been blessed with opportunities over four decades to study leadership as a student, to research leadership as an academic, to teach leadership as a professor, to observe leadership as a consultant, and to practice leadership as the person in charge.

I have always been, and still remain, very curious about how leaders, whether they function as front-line supervisors or seasoned corporate heads, exert their influence over others.

While I appreciate the numerous theories and published empirical studies on leadership, my main interest is to identify the practical differences between leaders who succeed and leaders who fail in the daily execution of their duties.

While leadership has still not evolved to a pure science, this book records leadership practices that I believe are successful for most leaders, in most situations, most of the time.

I deeply appreciate the following leaders who have allowed me up-close-and personal-views of how effective leadership can impact organizations. These vast experiences have expanded my understanding of nuanced leadership dynamics in ways that are simply not possible through research and study: Lynne Aston, Vice President of Human Resources of Viega LLC, Dr. Ely Bartal, Chief Executive Officer of Kansas Surgery and Recovery Hospital, the late W. Frank Barton, Co-founder of Rent-A-Center and namesake of the Barton School of Business, Dr. Donald Beggs, former president of Wichita State University, Barry Downing, founder and former president of Corporate Lodging Consultants, Dr. Gregory Duick, President, Chairman and Co-founder of the Kansas Heart Hospital, Kim Fanning, Senior Vice

President Education and Training, Presbyterian Manors of Mid-America, Julian Guerra II, President, Perfekta Aerospace, Mary Herrin, former President of the Central Association of College and University Business Officers, Al Higdon, co-founder of Sullivan, Higdon and Sink Advertising Agency, Dr. Eugene Hughes, former president of Wichita State University, Professor Fran Jabara, Former Dean of the W. Frank Barton School of Business and founder of the Center for Entrepreneurship, Jim Jones, former Director of the Kansas Department of Transportation, Mary Rapp MacBain, President/CEO of the Kansas Society of CPAs, the late Mike Oatman, co-founder and CEO of Great Empire Broadcasting, Inc., Dan Ramlow, Executive Vice President of the Kansas Contractors Association, the late Darrel Rolph, former CEO and founder of Carlos O'Kelly's Mexican Food Restaurants, Howard Sherwood, Chairman Emeritus, Sherwood Construction Company, Doug Sterbenz, Executive Vice President and Chief Operating Officer of Westar Energy, and John Walters, former president of Walters-Morgan Construction Company.

I am deeply grateful to the following individuals who have successfully and creatively promoted my workshops and appearances: the late Dr. Sam Bruno, former Director of the Center for Advanced Management Programs, University of Houston at Clear Lake, Susan Cherches, former Director of the Center for Management Development, Wichita State University, Eugene Dombrowski, former Vice President of The Dartnell Corporation, and especially Pat McLeod, Director of the Center for Management Development, Wichita State University.

I also very much appreciate the expert professional editing of the manuscript by Denise Rhoades, the design work of Jim L. Friesen, and the publishing assistance of Judy Entz.

Table of Contents

Chapter 1: New

✦

(The good news is, "I got the promotion.")

The differences between doing a job yourself and leading others are as different as night and day.

I recall, many years ago, when I accepted my first real management position. I had a doctoral degree in organizational behavior and I had published a bushel of articles and books on management and leadership. In short, I was totally unprepared.

There is an old expression that says, "You can never know what a person is really like unless you are married to him." I think you can paraphrase this to read, "You can never really know what a person is like until he works for you." It also works to say, "You can never know what a person is really like until you work for him."

The move from employee to manager offers particularly unique challenges, but anyone moving to any new position faces some of the same challenges.

A. Three Ways Leading Differs from Doing

As the old saying goes, "Yesterday I couldn't even *spell* supervisor. Now, I *are* one."

We promote people to management positions with little thought of the difference between doing and managing.

Respond "yes" or "no" to the following:

Can you…
1. Tolerate a lot of loose ends?

2. Handle people getting angry with you?
3. Speak your mind when others disagree?
4. Get satisfaction from the accomplishments of others?
5. Support upper management against employee complaints?

"Yes" answers suggest that you can handle some of the major differences between doing work and leading others.

Why do people get promoted? They did a good job as an employee; they did not miss work; and they got along reasonably well with others.

However, the very things that make a person successful as an employee might actually get in the way of succeeding as a manager.

Employees Do a Job: Leaders Get Others to Do a Job

Successful employees are diligent and impatient. They accomplish something tangible every day at work. Employees do not have to worry about much more than doing their own jobs.

Many managers fail because they approach management the same way they did their "doing" jobs. When a problem raises its ugly head, they simply jump into the fray and do the work themselves.

An employee of a mediocre manager said, "When we get behind, I don't worry. I know the manager is going to roll up his sleeves and help us. He will stay as late as it takes."

Such actions may sometimes be necessary, but it is not the manager's job to do the work.

Employees' Days are Predictable: Leadership is Messy

A manager described his day, "Today, I had two people absent, an upset customer, two other employees who had a misunderstanding with each other, a meeting that went on too long, and a new employee who is making too many mistakes. I just didn't get a thing done all day. I'll be glad when things get back to normal."

But that is normal. There are always loose ends, things to fix, schedules to change, meetings to attend, and unexpected "potholes" to worry about.

Employees are Fulfilled by Tasks: Leaders are Fulfilled by Team Building

"As an employee, even when I had a tough day, I could go home in the evening knowing that I had done a good job," explained a new manager. "It gave me a sense of satisfaction."

"As a manager," she said, "I seem to spend all day listening, explaining, correcting, changing, adjusting, tolerating, and worrying. Often, I feel like I didn't get a thing done!"

But that is what managers do. And it does not get any better after a year or two or ten.

B. When You Move into a Leadership Position, Start off "Tough"

"Everyone was very complimentary to me when they learned that I was to be the new departmental director," reported a recently promoted leader.

"And I noticed," the new leader continued, "during the first few weeks people were on very good behavior. Staff members who were typically slow met their deadlines. Those who made mistakes got things correct. Even the one with a habit of being late started showing up on time."

The leader explained further that prior to her appointment; the department had been performing like an eighth place team in an eight-team league.

"I thought that I was going to have to make a lot of changes," she said. "But my staff responded so well that I relaxed."

The leader was in a very pronounced "honeymoon" phase of her transition. After about five months, this phase started turning ugly. Low-performing staff members returned to their old and inefficient habits.

The leader talked with the disappointed producers, inquired if there were problems, and encouraged them to improve.

Most responded with anger or feigned hurt. They could not understand why the leader was disappointed. After all, they had been very supportive of her.

The new leader was perplexed. She wondered what she had done. Just when things seemed to be going so well, for no apparent reason, the wheels started wobbling.

The leader's decisions and actions in the first days of a new assignment set the tone for months, perhaps years.

Start as a Hard Nose

Leaders who are very supportive and accommodating at the start of their tenures have a hard time "getting tough" when they need to.

"You started out like you were going to be nice, but after awhile you turned out just like the rest of them," is the way a subordinate described a leader who started easy.

Leaders who loosen up after a demanding start are more likely to generate comments like, "I thought you were going to be hard to work for but you've really turned out to be very effective."

Make Key Decisions Quickly

Identify key decisions and make them early. To determine what decisions you should make, evaluate:

1. **Personnel.** If you think you need to make personnel changes, make them sooner rather than later. In this process, treat all staff members with dignity.
2. **Work quality.** If work quality and accuracy need improving, establish your expectations during the first few days on the job.
3. **Work quantity.** Is the work being done on time? Do reports meet the deadline? Are you delivering enough products (services)? Be specific.
4. **Policies.** Are staff members following departmental policies regarding attendance, safety, and the like? Spell out policies you intend to enforce.

If you are dissatisfied with performance or behavior in any of these four areas, make changes and make them quickly.

I do not suggest an arrogant, know-it-all approach to making corrections. Talk with people. Listen to suggestions. Be considerate. But do something.

Embrace Your Technology

Technology is here to stay. Keep up with it! If you do not fully understand your department's use of technology, do your homework. Take a cram course. Ask your technology experts to help you.

It is not necessary to be the departmental expert, but you need to understand how your department uses technology. You also need to take the lead in proposing technology changes and upgrades.

A lack of appreciation for, or knowledge of, technology has become the wrecking ball of a lot of today's leaders.

New leaders who get off to great starts are more likely to have successful finishes.

C. Six Things You Might Have Done as an Employee that You Cannot Do as a Leader

Do you lose your temper on the job?

Do you resist changes made by higher management?

Do you pass the buck to higher management for decisions you do not agree with?

Do you vent your frustrations in front of your staff members?

These are a few of the things that you lose the right to do if you wish to be an effective leader.

"I knew my life was going to be different when I became a supervisor," explained a newly promoted employee. "But I just didn't know how it was going to be different."

The supervisory job is not just a little different from that of an employee; it is as different as the North Pole and the Equator.

You might have gotten by with some things as an employee that you cannot allow yourself to do if you want to be successful in a leadership position. For instance, do not:

1. **Lose your temper.** Unless they punch someone or throw a computer through the plate glass window, employees probably do not disrupt work too much when they lose their tempers. But as a leader, your loss of temper vibrates throughout the work group—maybe even for days.
2. **Resist upper management's changes.** As a leader, your job is to implement changes that your upper-level managers make. If you disagree with the change, tell your manager. But when you come out of your boss's office, your job is to "sell" the change.
3. **Pass the buck to the home office.** To be an effective leader, you have to commit to the mission and strategies of upper management. Resist the

urge to blame them for policies that your people do not like. Ask your people to follow the policies because you personally believe in them.

4. **Vent frustrations to your staff.** Avoid making comments to your team such as, "I don't like this any better than you do. It is not my idea. The people in Chicago must have their head buried somewhere in the desert." Such comments only reduce your credibility as a leader.

5. **Get even with a staff member.** At some time, a staff member, a peer, someone in another department, or a boss will wrong you. This is a guarantee. Deal with the issue appropriately, but resist the urge to record the incident in your memory for later payback. You cannot do your job well if you have to keep track of all of the unfair treatments bestowed upon you.

6. **Act as one of the gang.** You are never *not* the supervisor. If you want to test this, make a fool out of yourself some Saturday night in front of your employees. See how long it takes for the word to get back to work.

Supervisory and management jobs are very demanding. In a sense you are in "no man's land."

You do not sit in on the strategic discussions with upper management and you probably do not feel totally comfortable in their territories. Yet, you are no longer "one of the group."

Most supervisors have a sense of being caught in the middle. They know that they are supposed to execute upper management's plans. At the same time they often empathize with the feelings and frustrations of their employees.

But supervision is a critically important position. For most rank and file employees, their supervisor, for all practical purposes, *is* the company. How supervisors act and communicate has a great influence on whether employees will be happy and productive at work.

D. How a New Leader Should Handle Employees Who are Much Younger, Older, and Other Issues

The first few weeks, or even months, in a new position are usually exciting. Subordinates are supportive, peers are positive and bosses are trusting.

After the break-in period, subordinates begin questioning the new leader's authority. Unfortunately, many leaders allow subordinates to manipulate them.

Even confident leaders worry about their ability to handle certain situations. Leaders reveal their doubts by asking others how to deal with these issues. The six most common questions from new leaders that I receive are:

1. **How should a younger supervisor handle older, more experienced employees?** "I'm only 33," explained a new manager. "Many of my subordinates have been here a long time." The leader further explained that some employees were resisting her suggestions. "They say things like, 'When you've been here awhile longer, you'll learn not to take these things so seriously.'"

2. **How do you supervise staff members who are much younger than you?** "Most of the people we hire are very young," reported a new boss. "I'm not sure that I understand them very well. They don't seem too worried about whether they even have a job. If I ask them to do something they don't want to do, some will just refuse to do it."

3. **How do you lead people who you used to work with?** "I worked with them for five years," said the new leader. "It's hard for them to accept me as their boss." The leader thought that subordinates did not take her requests as seriously because they had known her as one of them.

4. **How does an outsider get the confidence of the group?** A new manager said, "Since I came from outside the company, my people do not think that I understand the culture here." The manager believed that staff members sometimes resisted his ideas because he did not have personal knowledge of decisions made during the last 10 years.

5. **How does a man lead a department of mostly women?** "They think I don't understand them," commented a new male supervisor. He admitted that he lacked confidence in dealing with his staff, especially when they disagreed with him.

6. **How do you get a department of men to accept a woman as their leader?** "I'm in a traditional male profession," reported a new boss. "All of my subordinates are men." The manager worried that she was not going to be able to gain the men's confidence enough for her to make changes.

When facing one or more of the challenges listed above consider the following.

One, it is normal for a few subordinates, sooner or later, to question the authority of the new boss. The only surefire way of discovering their limits is to test the leader.

Two, understand that when subordinates test your leadership, they select your least confident area. If you are young, they will blame their resistance on your youth; if you are older, subordinates will point this out to you; and so on.

The very same employees who complain about one person being too young will complain about another being too old, or too new, or not new enough, or a man, or woman.

Three, rather than try to figure out how to handle younger, older, former peers, and so on, simply do the right thing. If changes need to be made, make them. If a subordinate requires discipline, administer it. Do not lower your standards and do not alter your performance expectations.

Remember that you are now the leader. All leaders are in some ways different from their subordinates. Do not dwell on the differences.

E. When You Get Promoted,
Your Friends Will Treat You Differently

"I wonder if he is still going to be friends with us now that he is our new supervisor," commented an employee.

Seventy percent of the people that I survey in Supervisory Skills Workshops say that it is OK for a manager to maintain close friendships with subordinates.

Yet, 90 percent say that they have observed problems when managers associated on a regular basis with friends in their departments.

If two co-workers were friends and one got promoted, why should they terminate their friendship? Friends are rare and special. Even managers have a personal life.

As one said, "What I do own my on time and who I do it with is none of the company's business."

Technically, this statement may be true; but my observation is that it is very hard for a supervisor to maintain close, personal, off-the-job relationships with one or two subordinates.

"Friends" Cause Their Managers Problems

Here are the reasons friends cause problems for their managers.

One, other subordinates perceive favoritism whether it is accurate or not.

Two, it is almost impossible to keep from talking about work issues with your friends, even in a duck blind at 6:00 a.m. on a Saturday morning.

Three, even the most supportive of friends expect a favor now and then from the boss. After all, what are friends for?

Four, friendship relations complicate many decisions. For instance, assume that a friend and another subordinate are being considered for a new work assignment. Both are qualified and both want the position.

If the supervisor promotes his friend, others will say, "He got the position because they are friends."

But suppose the supervisor says to his friend, "I'm going to give the position to another person because I want to prove that I'm not showing favoritism to a friend."

What kind of friend would this supervisor be? Because they were friends, not because he lacked qualifications, he lost out on the position. Just remember, supervisors are never *not* the supervisor, no matter if an encounter is off the clock and off the premises. In this case, things that happen in Vegas do not stay in Vegas.

Accept Changes in Relationships with Friends

Of course, many new supervisors have personal friends among their former co-workers. How should they handle the relationship?

I do not suggest a dramatic fracturing of friendship behaviors. I do believe that, over time, the intensity of the relationships will and should change.

Perhaps the new supervisor can begin his tenure by saying to his friend, "There's a chance I'm going to be fully loaded with these new responsibilities. I know that you will understand that I may not have as much free time to spend with you."

The supervisor can also impress upon his friend that he will need his support. Most friends fully understand the pressures of a new position and they will be very supportive.

If they are not, there may be some question of how good a friend they really were.

A supervisory job requires a different focus and different responsibilities. Associations with other supervisors, additional obligations and concern with different issues will combine to leave less time for intense personal associations with subordinates.

F. Do Not Over Identify with Your Subordinates— You Are Now Part of the Leadership Team

"We've got a big problem," a new supervisor explained to his boss. "Some of my people are frustrated with the new work schedule because they will have to work Saturdays."

The distraught supervisor explained that he had talked with the agitated staff members and understood their concerns. "I just hope I can convince you," the supervisor reported to his manager, "to rethink this new schedule rotation."

In this case, after a thorough analysis including employee input, management decided to change work schedules. The change, they hoped, would offer services more convenient to their clients and hold down costs.

Management also understood that the new schedule would distress some employees; still leadership thought the change would give them an edge in their very competitive environment.

What is Over Identification with Subordinates?

Over identification simply means that when you are caught in the middle between your staff and your bosses, you side with your staff.

In the example above, the supervisor admitted, "Yes, I understand why management wants to make the change. I just believe that I have to stand up for my people."

Front-line managers routinely find themselves squeezed between upper management strategies and employee needs. As one supervisor said, "I know what management is trying to do, but they have forgotten what is like for the employees. If they would spend more time here, they would understand how the employees feel."

The concept of "supporting your people" is laudable. However, there is a higher concept operating here. It is the concept of "serving the organization's mission."

Yes, it is crucial for front-line managers to empathize with their people and help them satisfy their needs. But supervisors must never forget that their highest priority is to lead their people to accomplish the objectives of the organization.

Put differently, organizational objectives trump individuals' needs.

A Few Signs of Over Identification

You may be over identifying with staff if any of the following statements apply:

You...
- Always side with employees when they disagree with management decisions.
- Go to extraordinary efforts to help one employee adjust to a work demand.
- Awaken at night worrying about your subordinates' welfare.
- Worry excessively about how employees are going to handle a particular change.
- Significantly inconvenience the majority of your staff to accommodate a few.
- Cause hardships for other departments in taking care of your people.
- Believe that greed is the major reason for management's unpopular decisions.
- Consistently argue with higher management about their decisions.
- Continuously feel sorry for yourself and your staff.
- Overreact to perpetual whiners.
- Blame others—managers, competitors, vendors, designers, and the like—when your department fails to accomplish its objectives.

Because front-line managers are in daily, even hourly, contact with their subordinates, employees have ample opportunities to "sell" their frustrations. Upper management is more distant—both in space and in organizational culture. Thus, management's expressions do not hit supervisors with the same number of decibels as employee gripes.

When perplexed on what position to take, choose the one that best serves the organization's mission.

G. Four "Hidden" Challenges
of Moving from Worker to Leader

"I remember well when they told me that I was going to be the new supervisor," recalled an experienced manager. "I was excited but nervous. The vice president congratulated me. Employees were very supportive."

After ten years, though, the manager also remembers challenges that seemed to appear out of thin air. "Looking back," he said, "there are a few things I wish I had been aware of."

Your Former Co-workers Become Skeptical

"I was surprised," explained a new supervisor, "when some employees aimed the same complaints toward me as I had heard them lodge against headquarters. Some thought that I did not understand how our policies affected them. They just forgot that I had worked alongside them for more than six years."

As a new manager you may be the most caring person since Mother Teresa, but your employees have never been in management. It is impossible for some to understand management's perspective. You may be the same human being, but you have a different title, different responsibilities, and an altered orientation. This is enough to make some employees skeptical.

Your Work Habits Will Change

We are creatures of habit. We develop routines. We park in the same place, approach our work stations along the same path, rub elbows with the same people, go to lunch at the same places, and approach our jobs in the same manner.

In a new position, all of these routines are subject to change. A new supervisor said, "It was like the world started rotating in the opposite direction. Not quickly. Not dramatically. I would have thought these subtle changes wouldn't have mattered, but they were quite unnerving."

Your Employees Will Treat You Differently

Co-workers talk about different things. They may criticize an executive, whine about a policy, or bemoan the new initiative. When talking to each other, this is just talk—a way to relieve stress. But if the same words were spoken to management, they would take on a different meaning.

It is impossible to maintain the same relationships with subordinates as with co-workers. Employees want you to be their leader, not their buddy. Previous friends understand that you are now the boss. Some may even expect special favors but they will respect you more if you show no favoritism—not even to them.

You Will Feel the Pinch of Being in the Middle

Make no mistake, as a front-line supervisor, you are in the middle. You are responsible for carrying out the directives of higher managers who may seldom see or talk with your employees. Upper management cannot possibly be as aware of your employees' concerns as you are. You can see things in employees' faces, body language, and voice tones that are impossible to communicate to a manager in the main building or Toronto or Belgrade.

At the same time, employees cannot possibly see the same perspective as upper management. They were not in the meetings. They do not have the same pressures. They are not as aware of new pressures on the horizon or new competitors emerging from the dust.

What to do? One, do not be surprised by these subtleties. Two, do not take them personally. This is part of the adjustment process for everyone. Three, do not let these shake your confidence. Four, and most important, remember that you are there to get a job done. Deliver on the company's objectives. Enforce company policies. Do your staff a favor by being a firm and fair leader dedicated to serving your company's mission.

H. Identify "Keepers," "Movers," and "Removers" When Taking a New Position

"I was in the position for two weeks, and I knew something was bad wrong," explained a newly promoted manager. "I inherited two people with spirit-killing attitudes, a marginal performer who had retired on the job, and a couple of others who thought the company owed them a living."

Most managers, when they get a new position, feel a sense of pride and responsibility. And employees tend to be on their best behavior.

During this early phase, I think it is crucial to assess current personnel. Before you change anything else, you must know what you have in the way of personnel. No matter how good one's leadership skills may be, you can't effectively round up cattle on an ox. To be successful, you must have the right people on the team and in the right assignments.

Identify the Keepers, Movers and Removers

During the first two weeks on the job (it would be even better if you could do this prior to taking the job) make a complete evaluation of all inherited personnel. Consider separating them into three categories: keepers, movers and removers.

"Keepers" are the persons who are doing good work and fitting into the team. Keepers are proven performers. They know how to do their jobs. Other staff members respect them. Do whatever is necessary to keep these people on your team.

"Movers" are also good team players with talents, but they may not be in the right assignments. Other positions within the department may better suit their skills. Move them to other positions within the department, or redefine their jobs to fit their skills.

"Removers" represent staff members who are not contributing. Some may not have the skills to do their tasks. Others may be so cranky and whiney that no one can work with them. Unfortunately, you may inherit a staff member who is both inept and cranky.

Target these people for removal. I understand that you cannot fire "movers" your first day on the job. But you can avoid wasting a lot of time on training and elongated counseling and mentoring sessions. Further, you can accurately document performance records and policy violations to create grounds for eventual termination.

Use Data and Interviews as a Basis of Analysis

Use performance data and personal interviews to identify what category each staff member fits into.

Study performance appraisal files for the last three years. Careful reading can produce a lot of clues about staff members' contributions, or lack thereof. Check all other recorded performance data for individuals and the department.

After studying recorded data, sit down for an interview (plan on 30 to 60 minutes) with each employee. Ask questions like: "What about your job do you do well?" "What do you struggle with?" "What have you done to develop your skills during the past year?" "What do you consider your most important accomplishments?" "What have you been most disappointed in?" "Who do you work well with in the company?" "Who frustrates you the most?" "What suggestions do you have for dramatically improving the department?"

After each interview, make notes on what impressed you and what concerned you. When you finish these two processes, you should have a good picture of your team.

Do not look for upside. Do not look for potential. Do not look for needed improvements.

Accept the reality of what each individual has done. Do not even think about trying to mold the laggards into star performers. You will dramatically increase your odds for success if you keep the good employees, move good personnel who may be out of place, and professionally terminate nonperformers.

Chapter 2: Lead

✦

(Push, pull or get out of the way.)

Some leaders are big. Some are small. Some are loud. Some are quiet. Some are creative. Some are plodding. Leaders emerge from many different molds. Cookie cutter development programs do not produce leaders.

The possession of certain traits does not guarantee you to be a leader. Still, research and practical observations suggest that many leaders tend to exhibit common traits and behaviors.

Are you ready for a leadership role? What traits do followers want to see? How far will your technical expertise carry you? Are you a people person? Can you make it happen?

A. How to Tell if You are Ready for Leadership

Answer the following questions "yes" or "no."

1. Are you comfortable getting in front of people and talking?
2. Do you always do what you said you were going to do?
3. Can you remain calm when the wheels are falling off?
4. Can you keep a lot of balls in the air at the same time?
5. Do you like to help others get better?
6. Do you enjoy being in charge?
7. Do you frequently change things?
8. Can you let it "roll off your back" when someone gets angry with you?
9. Do you like a sense of adventure?
10. Do you get back on your feet quickly after failure?

Seven "yes" answers may suggest that you are ready to lead.

"My supervisor is going to retire later this year," confided an anxious employee. "I believe that I will be considered for the position. But I'm pretty young and I haven't been here as long as some."

The employee fretted that she may not be ready, that older employees might not accept her and younger employees might not take her seriously. She admitted that she would like to have the position but her self-doubts hung on her like a lead weight.

It is OK to be Nervous

New leadership responsibilities seem to fit some people like a comfortable pair of shoes. The person just seems right for the job.

In reality, no matter how confident a person appears to be, most new leadership responsibilities usually surface nagging doubts and simmering worries.

In short, it is OK to be nervous, worried and concerned when facing new leadership opportunities.

Are You Ready?

"But how can I tell if I am just trying to avoid risks or whether I'm really ready for the challenge?" asked the uncertain employee. "I think I can do it. But I sure don't want to fail."

We do not have blood tests that can predict whether a person is ready for a leadership position. But the ten items above can allow you to gauge your level of comfort. The higher your score, the more likely it is that you are ready.

Set Personal Development Goals

Be cautious though. A low score does not doom you to sub-par leadership. Likewise, a high score does not ensure hand-clapping success. But even if your real score is low, that is not a bad thing. All organizations need good followers.

Rather than assume a low score seals your fate, consider items that you answered "no" on to be goals for personal development.

For instance if you are not comfortable speaking in front of groups, work on public speaking skills. If you feel uncomfortable being in charge, volunteer for assignments. Take responsibility, perform successfully and increase your confidence. If it bothers you when people get angry with you, get over it.

Some people seem to naturally and easily exhibit these leadership readiness traits. But the good news is, even if the traits do not come naturally to you, you may have the underlying talent that makes it possible for you to develop them.

B. Effective Leaders Avoid the Alligators by Focusing on the Mission

"When you are up to your waist in alligators, it is hard to remember that your mission was to clean the swamp," commented a long ago wit.

Imagine this: With a considerable budget for equipment and labor, a team was sent out with the specific purpose of draining a swamp by a certain date.

The second day on the job, an employee raced into camp shouting, "There is an alligator out here as big as an elephant!" Everyone abandoned their work assignments and ran to look. As the crew stood gawking, half a dozen other alligators surfaced and gawked back at the onlookers.

The crew leader said, "There are probably a lot more where these came from. I guess we need to get them out of here." The leader recruited an expert alligator trapper who trained other members of the crew to find and remove alligators.

Within two days, the entire crew was busy finding and removing alligators. Toward the end of the week, a vice president visited the site and asked, "How are we progressing on our schedule to clean the swamp?"

"I'm happy to report that we have just about removed all of the alligators," replied the leader.

"But our mission here is to clean the swamp."

"Boss, when you are up to your neck in alligators, it is hard to focus on the mission."

Examples of Mission Distractions ("Alligators")

Unfortunately, real-life leaders waste assets struggling with "alligators" and get distracted from the mission.

I recall a leader who was given a tough assignment. After a couple of days on the job, employees' morale sank like a lead balloon and complaints came from everywhere. The morale issue became a distraction (an alligator).

The leader focused on documenting reasons that might prevent their success. He also spent money on retreats and other events to boost morale, diverting resources away from the real mission. The team failed to achieve the assignment and morale sank further.

Take another example: There are several documented cases of companies embracing programs (quality circles, total quality improvement, ISO 9000, Six Sigma) so vigorously they forget that their mission was to add value by delivering services to their customers.

One organization insisted that everyone be on a process-improvement team. The leader hired staff to train people, document team meetings, record attendance, and catalog team recommendations. Employees spent a lot of time deleting, adding and modifying processes. The company actually won an award for its efforts.

However, employees diverted so much resource to improving processes (the alligator); they had little time and energy left for serving their customers. Customer complaints increased. Profits declined.

Another company added to their performance evaluation system a requirement that managers implement elaborate personal development (PD) programs for all employees' weak areas. Staff devoted countless hours and created voluminous files for PD's for all employees. Two years later, overall company performance had actually declined. The PD programs (alligators) were abandoned.

I do not mean to imply that all efforts to improve morale, processes or employee development represent a misallocation of assets. I do emphasize that, whatever else you get involved in, always remember that your number one concern is to accomplish the mission.

C. The Most Important Leadership Trait is Integrity

The most important trait that followers want to see in their leaders is integrity—honesty, openness and straight-forwardness. Do what you say you are going to do. Tell people what is going on. Do not be aloof or secretive.

Integrity is more important than competence. It is more important than vision. It is more important than intelligence.

"If we can't trust you," commented an insightful employee, "It makes it hard for us to follow you into risky situations."

What Causes People to Distrust Their Leaders?

The most common cause of distrust is to misrepresent something. For example, a supervisor blamed a rotten decision on his boss. Later, employees discovered that it was the supervisor who actually made the decision.

Intent to mislead is another reason to distrust. In a tense discussion, an employee asked, "Is there any truth to the rumor that we are going to centralize purchasing in the home office and close our department?"

"There is no truth to that rumor," the manager boldly stated.

Three months later, the company newsletter announced that they were discussing the prospect of outsourcing their purchasing function.

The angry employees accosted their manager, "You told us that we were not going to lose purchasing. But our newsletter said that we were considering outsourcing it to another company."

"I told you the truth," explained the manager. "You asked me if we were going to centralize purchasing and I said, 'No.' No one asked me anything about outsourcing."

This manager may think that he technically told the truth, but employee trust went south faster than migrating ducks in advance of a cold front.

Withholding information also infringes on trust. Employees want to know everything that impacts their jobs. And they want to know it now!

When managers delay communicating any changes that impact employees' work lives, they engender distrust.

Surprises also poison trusting relationships. As youngsters, we may have enjoyed surprise birthday parties. But adults do not like to be surprised, not even when it is considered a "good" surprise.

"I would certainly prefer a good surprise to a bad surprise," explained an employee, "but my real preference is to have no surprise at all."

If you want to personally test the "surprise creates distrust theory," do not tell your spouse (or close relationship) that you will be working unusually late. Show up at home about 12 hours later than normally.

In addition to worry and perhaps anger, you will likely generate a huge dose of suspicion and distrust. Similar feelings occur at work when leaders surprise employees.

How to Maintain Trust

Integrity is fragile. It may take months to generate trust among some people. But just one misstep can destroy it in a nanosecond. Build integrity by avoiding the potholes of misrepresentation, allowing employees to arrive at false beliefs, withholding information, and surprising people.

Consistently and frequently communicate what is likely to happen in the work group. Anticipate what bothers people. Tell them what you know even if they did not know enough to ask the right question.

Prepare people for bad news and communicate all bad news early. If you think something might come as a surprise, prepare people ahead of time by honestly discussing possible options. At all times, be truthful with your staff. Be honest even when the truth scares people, makes them angry, or causes them to dislike you.

A good sign of integrity is to build a reputation so that employees say, "I may not always agree with my leader, but I always know where she stands and what she thinks."

D. Why Leaders Must Have Character to Succeed

"What is the purpose of leaders?"

"What is character?"

"How does character impact leadership?"

Leaders Have Real Impact on Companies

Unlike the comment from an unidentified wit, leaders do more than find a parade and jump in front of it.

Good leaders paint visions of the future for their followers. Good leaders also listen to followers as they tweak their visions.

Leaders have influence. Skillful leaders use their sway to gain commitment to group goals that serve the common good.

Bad leaders also have influence. But they use their cunning to serve their personal interests, usually at the expense of their followers.

Companies need leaders to influence 10 (or 10,000) people to work as a team toward shared purposes.

Leaders Who Have Character, Consistently Do the Right Thing

According to noted author, Francis Fukuyama, character is the ability to do the right thing under trying circumstances. (Will I tell the truth when it is not to my benefit?)

Intellectually, it is often easy to know the right thing to do. It may be hard to actually do the right thing. People who consistently do the right things, even when it is tough to do so, have character.

Character is a product of our habits. We develop most of these habits in our early childhood. As children, we hear from our parents, "I want you to tell me the truth, now." From teachers we hear, "I do not allow cheating in my classes." Religions teach us standards like the Ten Commandments.

Of course, no human is error free, but high-character leaders misstep only very rarely. Leaders of low character make deceit a way of life.

Leaders Who Lack Character Often Destroy Their Companies

Leaders who lack character frequently do the wrong things—lie, cheat, steal, manipulate, deceive. They know the right thing to do; they just do not do it. Why? They lack character.

Leaders who are deficient in character have a dire, negative impact upon followers.

- First, "trust"—the glue that makes it possible to coordinate complex behaviors—goes away. Followers distrust their leader and each other.
- Second, the blame game emerges. The leader blames outside forces. Then the leader blames followers. Followers aim blame back toward the leader. Thus, leader "bad behaviors" encourage a downward spiraling of follower "bad behaviors."
- Third, because leaders lose their ability to influence through respect, they resort to exaggerated punishments and rewards to keep followers in line. Leaders publicly criticize (demote, transfer, terminate) followers who do not support the king. Obedient followers receive much-desired rewards (lavish praise, promotions, bonuses, pay increases).
- Fourth, although it may take some time, civility and respect dissipates. A "What's in it for me?" attitude develops and the organization loses its competitive edge.

Unfortunately, leaders who lack character seldom change their ways—even when rodents begin fleeing the ship.

At this point, followers have only two viable alternatives: (1) purge the "bad apple" from leadership, or (2) allow individuals to raid what's left of the company's treasures before it goes out of business.

E. Successful Leadership Requires Much More than Technical Ability

"Sam was a good employee," explained his regional manager. "He had great technical expertise and he worked hard. Didn't say too much, but everybody respected him. When a supervisory position came open, I selected Sam. Guess what? It turned out to be a very bad decision."

The manager further explained that Sam had very little patience for subordinates who could not quickly fix their mistakes. After a few months, employees commented that, "Sam has let his new title go to his head."

Sam also appeared frustrated. He became exasperated when employees were not doing their work quite right. He would push them aside and finish it himself.

Lose a Good Employee and Gain a Poor Manager

Its conventional wisdom, and common knowledge, that we tend to promote our best technical employees into managerial positions.

Intuitively, it makes sense to reward your best technical performers by promoting them. They usually get a pay raise and a title which connotes higher status. Such promotions also send others the message that "good work is rewarded around here."

We should not assume, though, that employees who are good at doing things well will also be good leaders. Is it possible for employees with outstanding technical skills to make good leaders? The answer is, "Yes, of course they can." But many do not. Others eventually "get it" after wobbling around for awhile.

The Challenge for Technical Experts

Good technical specialists—engineers, accountants, computer jocks, financial analysts, and statistical experts—are more likely to have introvert personalities.

Introverts prefer to work alone. They revel in painstaking details, meaningful paperwork, and tedious activities, i.e. precision. Even small movements of the "needle" keep them energized. They have the ability to focus for hours while dislodging meaningful data from tangled heaps.

Ambiguity and clutter motivates introvert specialists to find clean-burning solutions. The gold at the end of the rainbow for many skilled performers is "the perfect part," "the ultimate design," "the cover-all-bases analysis," "the perfect solution."

The very traits that make experts successful in doing what they do actually get in the way of transitioning into leadership positions. The expert's work world values precision, order and logic. By contrast, a leader's role is often messy, herky-jerky and ambiguous. Further, the sense of pride and fulfillment associated with doing a tangible task well is missing.

Relationship complexities are more dynamic and unexplainable than task complexities. Successful leaders have to account for distasteful political relationships, egos, pride, insecurities, envy, hurt feelings, petty conflicts and even childish behaviors.

How to Transition from Technical Jobs to Leadership

Technical experts, who successfully transition into effective leadership, realize that they must learn how to get others to do the work. With their eyes on the company goal, leaders learn to rely more on their instincts, insights and intuitions.

Leaders solve the puzzle of what makes each of their subordinates tick. They learn when to push, when to back off, when to be tolerant, when to explain and when to demand. Leaders know which subordinates respond to praise and which respond to scolding.

By understanding the egos of human relations, leaders get a feel for things in a way that is quite different from the logical analysis of technical performers.

Some outstanding technical performers may not have the personality or the desire to learn to rely on the mushy aspects of leadership. For these, it may be better to find ways to continuously reward their performance rather than pushing them into leadership.

Rational analysis is very necessary for leadership. It is just not sufficient.

F. How to Focus on Tasks and People at the Same Time

"I don't have the power to fire people," exclaimed a frustrated manager, "so I really can't get my subordinates to do things they don't really want to do."

It is true that if a leader had a big enough gun and was willing to use it, she could get her staff to do most anything. Or, if a leader had all of the gold in the pot at the end of the rainbow and was willing to bribe people, she could get people to do a lot of things they might not really want to do.

Fortunately, we do not allow leaders to use guns, and very few have enough gold (or authority to use money) in any significant way. Still, it is the leader's job to influence people—to work fast, to work accurately, to follow policies and to help each other.

I observe many leaders who influence people without force or money. How do they do it? Basically, they use their personal relationships with subordinates. Think of a two-dimensional relationship: people and task.

Do You Put People First?

A leader should know whether a staff member's child won the weekend soccer game without having to ask. Highly effective leaders care about their staff members as persons. The relationship is not contrived. Leaders truly care.

Without crossing privacy boundaries, people-oriented leaders understand family situations, hobbies, and personal preferences. They understand when employees face joy or worry in their personal lives.

People leaders also ask employees' opinions on matters at work. And employees can answer, "Strongly agree" to the question, "Do my opinions at work really count?"

People leaders want their employees to mature, to grow and to improve their skills. Such employees report, "My leader cares about me as a person." Employees of people leaders will also say they "very frequently" receive words of praise and appreciation from their bosses.

Patience, support, understanding, concern, listening, empathy and appreciation are the ingredients from which leaders construct their people skills.

Do You Put Tasks First?

Effective leaders also clearly communicate the importance of accomplishing company objectives and embracing policies. This is the task part of the relationship.

Task leaders make it easy for employees to confidently state, "I know exactly what is expected of me at work, and I know exactly where I stand."

Task leaders measure performances and frequently give feedback. As a task leader explained, "I want my employees to know within two decimal places how well they are doing."

Should employee performance wane or behavior bump against key policies, a task leader is quick to express, "Frankly, I'm disappointed. I really do expect you make the deadline. And 'yes' I insist that you follow all safety policies."

Repeated subordinate failures bring more severe warnings, including written reprimands, perhaps even a recommendation of termination.

The better leaders avoid the either/or trap of identifying themselves as either a high task or a high people leader. Rather they see themselves as high task and high people, both at the same time.

When employees do the right things, leaders lean heavily on the people part. When employees stray, leaders are quick to exert their task dimension.

G. Real Leaders Make It Happen

"All of my days are completely filled with appointments and meetings," complained a manager. "I have to come before office hours or take things home to get my work done."

"Who handles your schedule?" I asked.

"I have an excellent secretary who controls my calendar," he responded.

Further investigation revealed that the secretary simply scheduled every request by staff and others to see the manager. This manager is no doubt busier than bees during nectar-gathering time, but he is not leading.

Leaders initiate actions! Set the agendas! Do things! Organize the efforts of others! Leader action is necessary to efficiently chase a vision.

Do You Initiate More Actions than You Respond to?

You may find it interesting to check your initiate-to-response ratio. How many times do you act to cause something to happen versus the times that you respond to others' requests?

A low ratio suggests a responding, reacting, passive, non-leading approach. By contrast, a high ratio describes an action-oriented leader.

Do You Make More Phone Calls than You Receive?

Most of us engage in dozens of communication episodes each day. Pick a day and simply count a few events.

How many phone calls (faxes, emails) did you place? Receive? For example, assume that you placed 15 phone calls and received 30, giving you a ratio of 1 to 2—a low ratio.

An example of a high ratio would be 30 calls placed and 10 calls received—3 to 1. Real leaders tend to have high ratios—they initiate more communication than they respond to.

How Many Meetings Do You Call?

Leaders call meetings and leaders attend meetings. What is your ratio of meetings called to meetings attended?

For a more in-depth analysis, count the agenda items of meetings that you attended last week. Compare the number of agenda items that you provided to the items that others put on the agenda. Is your ratio high or low?

How Many Changes Do You Initiate?

Change percolates around us all of the time. Much of the time people simply respond by complaining about the changes suggested by others. How many changes in policies, procedures, techniques, and methods did you suggest last week?

Leaders initiate changes. They take risks. Leaders consistently search for better, more effective ways of doing things. Their ratio of ideas proposed to ideas received is high.

Recently, I asked a leader if she ever proposed new ways of doing things to her bosses. "All of the time," she responded.

Are your ideas ever rejected?" I continued.

"Yes, all of the time."

"What do you do when your bosses reject one of your suggestions?"

"I don't even get warmed up," she said, "until I get half-dozen rejections for the same idea."

In short, leaders are active people with active minds who take reasonable risks by frequently suggesting new ways.

While real leaders are very attentive to subordinate inputs, they avoid simply checking the wind before making every decision, responding only to straw polls, or staking out middle-of-the-road positions on complex issues.

As one leader put it, "I don't want to fail as a leader because I responded to someone else's ideas that I only half-heartedly believed in. If I crash, it will be because I vigorously pursued ideas that I personally believed in."

H. Provide High Performance Leadership

Identify whether you tend to agree or disagree with the following:

The Greatest Corporate Leaders:
1. Develop a clear vision prior to putting their team together.
2. Have a load of charisma.
3. Focus more on what to do than what not to do.
4. Expend a lot time and energy motivating people.
5. Rely heavily upon consensus decision making.

Most organizational leaders do a pretty good job. It is true that a few turn out to be flaming disasters. But most are pretty effective.

Yet, few leaders rise to the level of greatness. Few perform at record levels. Few soar with the eagles. How do these extraordinary leaders differ?

Author Jim Collins and his research team, in his best seller, *GOOD TO GREAT*, document how the companies that make the leap to "great" differ from the "merely good."

1. People Before Vision

Contrary to popular thought, the leaders in Collins' research concentrated on putting their team together before worrying about the vision.

As Collins put it, "...first get the right people on the bus, the wrong people off the bus, and the right people in the right seats—and then figure out where to drive it."

Great leaders know that it is critical to get talented people—people who can do things well. Once these talented people are on the bus, their insights also help the leader evolve the vision.

As the former great basketball coach of UCLA, John Wooden, explains, "Not every coach with good talent wins, but every coach who wins has good talent."

2. Modest and Fearless Versus Dynamic and Exciting

Modest, fearless, willful, humble, shy, understated, and gracious, were adjectives more likely to be descriptive of Collins' great leaders.

Leaders who are dynamic, articulate, exciting, strong, and larger than life do get the boldest print in the media and the most coverage on television. In fact, some become mega personalities on par with rock stars.

And charismatic leaders can be successful. But the truly great leaders tend to be more humble.

3. Decide What Not to Do

Great leaders reduce, downsize, sell off, or eliminate all of the many things that may be fun, interesting and exciting, but are not done very well.

As Collins said, "The good-to-great companies focused on those activities that ignited their passion."

The principle is to be honest about what you are good at doing. What can you potentially do better than other organizations?

Great leaders are clear about what they are not going to do.

4. Don't Try to Motivate People

Great leaders do not hire lazy, self-serving, arrogant, hostile employees and spend a lot of time and energy trying to turn them into committed, passionate, driven, cooperative team players.

Of course, leaders need motivated people. How do they get them? They hire them.

5. Make the Decision

Great leaders do seek the counsel of their staff members. They are open to input, and they seriously consider other's recommendations.

But the best leaders do not seek consensus. They recognize that consensus decisions are often not the most intelligent decisions.

A great leader, upon receiving a strong opposing view from a staff member responded, "Your view may have merit, but if I fail, I will fail doing what I strongly believe in."

With the greatest leaders, the final decisions remain with the leader.

Great leaders tend to be bold and humble, passionate and shy, willful and gracious—traits that produce great things while at the same time endearing them to their followers.

Chapter 3: Vision

❖

(Leaders Communicate the Big Picture.)

Vision and mission are ways that leaders communicate the big-picture purpose of the organization.

Vision represents what leaders think their organization can become. Mission describes what the organization does, its reason for being. Visionary leaders inspire others to commit to the vision while serving the mission.

A. How to Tell if You are a Visionary Leader

Check all of the following that describe you.

1. I am inspired by challenges.
2. I relentlessly believe in my vision.
3. Some people have described my zeal as "evangelistic."
4. When the opportunity presents itself, I go for it.
5. I have the courage to pursue high-risk strategies.
6. People say I am never satisfied with my accomplishments.
7. I have a stable set of core values.

All of the above are characteristics of leadership vision.

Henry Ford's vision was to build a motorcar that the masses could afford. Dr. Edwin Land passionately pursued his dream of photo cameras that could develop film inside the camera. Although turned down by all of the major camera manufacturers, Dr. Land lived to see his vision materialize.

What sets these visionary leaders apart from the crowd? Authors James C. Collins and Jerry L. Porras, in their excellent book, BUILT TO LAST, give us the answer. For six years, they studied successful companies. They also studied the also-rans.

Visionary Leaders Pursue Big Goals

Visionary leaders chase *Big Hairy Audacious Goals* (bee-hags). They do not play around with minor two to three percent improvements. As the old saying goes, "They back their ears and go for it!"

Bee-hags, although not always "realistic," inspire people. Bee-hags focus and compel; people commit to bee-hags. John Kennedy's "land a man on the moon and return him safely within this decade," was a high-flying, bee-hag. So was Wal-Mart's "$1 billion company in four years."

Visionary Leaders Build Distinctive Cultures

Employees either love or hate visionary leaders. And, "If you don't sing in tune according to their gospel, you are out of here!"

For example:

"Prove yourself at every level or leave"—Nordstrom.
"Wholesomeness…magic…clean-cut zealots." —Disneyland.
"Mormon-influenced, clean living, dedicated to service"—Marriott.

Visionary Leaders Act!

Strategic planning is OK. Opportunistic trial and error is better. Keep the successes, cut the failures—"Branching and pruning," as Johnson and Johnson's calls it.

Marriott got into prepackaged boxed lunches for airlines because customers kept buying snacks on the way to their planes and stuffing them in their pockets.

When two-tone paint jobs on automobiles became popular, available tapes allowed colors to run. In response, 3M invented masking tape. Later, because of requests for waterproofing tapes, 3M birthed scotch tape.

Visionary Leaders Promote Their Own

Visionary leaders take care of their own. They waste little time scouring the country in a search for the best person.

Powerhouse companies promote from within so they can provide a compass of core values to the next generation. Striving wannabes also know that they can achieve fame and promotions without having to leave the company. Continuity of leadership excels.

From 1806 to 1992, according to the research of Collins and Porras, only two visionary leaders (11% of their sample) hired CEOs from the outside. By comparison, 72% of the comparison companies hired from the outside.

Visionary Leaders Always Want to Get Better!

Benchmarking? Quarterly comparisons? Annual growth? Finally, success! Nah! Rather, it's always, "How can we be better tomorrow?" Resting on laurels? Comfort? Never! Not when a visionary leader is in charge.

Visionary leaders do not exit to a planning retreat to write their vision statements. Their visions are engrained within their being. Such leaders do not have to rely on superhuman discipline to chase their dream.

The dream is so much a part of their being it compels them to chase. How else could visionary leaders persist against all odds when most feedback tells them that they are going to fail?

B. The Role of a Mission Statement is to Keep Everyone Focused on Your Purpose

"I've got to run," said a manager. "We're having a meeting to rewrite our mission statement. It's our fourth rewrite."

Surveys suggest that 9 out of 10 companies have written mission statements. But the question is "How many of these mission statements are useful and meaningful?"

In my experience, the answer is, "Not many." In fact, I suggest that less than half of mission statements are meaningful. Further, some companies with good mission statements do not use them.

What is a Mission Statement?

A mission statement is a brief explanation of what a group does. It answers the questions, "Who are we?" "Why do we exist?" "What do we do?" The mission explains the company's reason for being.

Although companies answer these questions in different ways, I believe that mission statements, as a minimum, should:

- Define who the organization serves (customer, clients, patients, students),
- Identify products or services that the organization produces, and
- Describe the geographical location of operations (local, national, worldwide).

For example, an excerpt from a mission statement of a private, secondary military school reads,

"...*to provide Cadets, from throughout the nation, with the opportunity to grow spiritually, morally, intellectually and physically in a structured environment.*"

Effective Mission Statements are Brief, Active and Timely

It is not necessary to spend dozens of hours quibbling over mission phrasing and punctuation. The mission explains why an organization exists. It does not report all of the company's values, objectives and strategies.

There is little agreement among the experts on exactly how to write effective mission statements. Below are my suggestions:

1. **Be brief.** Short mission statements are better. They are easier to understand and easier to remember. I have read mission statements that have rambled on for a page or more. I think leaders should be able to describe their mission in one or two sentences.

2. **Use verbs.** Verbs connote action. They tell people what you do. Use them. I like words like: "build," "deliver," "manufacture," "sell," "distribute," "provide," and "create."

   For example the mission of Newport Shipping Company reads, "We will build great ships—at a profit if we can, at a loss if we must—but we *will* build great ships!"

3. **Minimize adjectives and adverbs.** Adjectives and adverbs add little value. Words like "high-quality," "the best," "excellent," "Number one," and "outstanding." These words are OK, but they have been used so much they are trite. Also, they do not say anything unique about the company.

   Take the following statement: "Our mission is to be the best in the industry by providing high-quality service to a wide-range of customers."

Or, "…to serve our customers by adding value with a commitment to continuous improvement."

These statements could accurately describe thousands of different companies in dozens of different industries. Still, with all of their glorified words, they reveal almost nothing about the companies.

4. **Keep the meaning timely.** While strategies and actions may change often, missions are more consistent. A good mission statement should serve for several years.

Mission Statements Differ from Slogans

Slogans are easy-to-remember phrases that remind us of a particular company. They are extremely effective in advertising but they are not, in my opinion, mission statements.

Some currently popular slogans include: "To solve unresolved problems," "Ladies and gentlemen serving ladies and gentlemen," "We are a diverse entertainment enterprise," or "To make people happy."

I do not criticize leaders for developing and promoting these slogans. I simply contend that slogans, no matter how effective, are not the same as mission statements.

Mission statements are valuable because they become anchors for decision-making. Leaders should evaluate all objectives and all strategies on how well they serve the mission.

C. Leaders Commitment to Mission is Greater than their Commitment to People

The mission! The mission! The mission! That is what we should care about.

An organization exists to do something--to build products, to deliver services.

Departments also have missions. They have a purpose—prepare reports, order things, keep records, assist managers, promote products.

The mission is simply the intent of the group, its reason for being. The mission of NASA is, "To explore, use, and enable the development of space for human enterprise." Walt Disney's mission is, "To make people happy."

Able Leaders Place Mission Ahead of People Issues

Missions trump individual needs. But some leaders mistakenly place individual needs above their mission, as in, "Morale is our most important concern."

If you think that high morale is the major concern of a leader, assume that customers decline by fifty percent. When the boss (or an investor or a donor) asks about your tanked performance, try responding, "But our morale is the highest it has ever been."

Some leaders overly identify with their people to such an extent that they find it hard to discipline employees who are obviously letting their team down.

Mission-challenged leaders will not terminate subordinates, even when they have retired on the job. They even fear asking the local whiner to take a turn at an undesirable task because it would upset him.

Resist the Temptation to Put People Ahead of Mission

The temptation to prioritize people over mission is understandable.

Leaders have an inherited need to earn acceptance and love from their followers. But followers have the ability to get mad. They cry. They criticize. They shun. They praise. They ignore. They get their feelings hurt. They mutiny.

Missions are intangible. They do not shout, argue, complain or ignore. In fact, leaders can trample a mission into mush without immediate retaliation from the mission.

It's a natural to want to avoid hurting or angering staff members, and some leaders achieve this by sacrificing commitment to their mission.

How to Keep Mission a Priority

To keep mission a top priority, leaders:

1. Closely identify with the mission. If leaders do not put the mission ahead of their personal desires for such things as popularity, promotions, friendships, and even earnings, they cannot rightfully expect their followers to properly identify with the mission.
2. Measure progress toward mission. Focus on a few, specific measures that chart progress toward mission. Measures may include sales, returns, deadlines, accuracy reports, customer satisfaction, budget, and the like.

3. Publicize measures. Convert the data into charts and graphs. Display the "pictures" of progress toward mission. Discuss them in regular meetings.

4. Use rewards and sanctions. Distribute lavish praise and bonuses to group members when they "take a giant step" toward the mission. Withhold privileges when they fumble and stumble.

5. Accept social pressure. Understand that when subordinates expend energies near their max they begin to resist. Not only do they balk, they may disagree, criticize, complain and avoid social interactions with their leader.

While there are temptations for leaders to sacrifice mission, there exists a stronger motivation to serve the mission.

Recall that the mission is the purpose for an organization's existence. Thus, if an organization does not serve its purpose, it eventually goes away. Dying companies, no matter how well intentioned, do not benefit people.

By contrast, groups that successfully serve their missions have the wherewithal to fulfill many human needs. Mission first, people second. This is the job of leadership.

D. How to Handle the Competition between Mission and Individual Needs

What does a leader do when the scales are equally balanced between serving the needs of the individual and the company?

Most leaders understand the need for balancing company demands with the need for employees to have a life as evidenced by the popular slogan, "God first, family second, the company third."

While many of us likely agree with the priority of these items, sometimes both the demands of the company and the family seem paramount. They tie as in "dead heat."

What to do when Individual Needs Compete with Company Mission

For instance, because of weather problems, electrical utility lines were down. To reinstall the services, many employees would be required to work overtime, including weekends, through an important holiday period.

Should the leader honor the customers' needs and keep many employees away from their families during an important holiday period? Would it be better to let the customers howl?

Take another example. For several months, a single mother had scheduled to visit a university orientation program with her daughter. The university had a policy of not rescheduling these meetings.

As part of a reorganization, the company rejiggered employee work schedules. The single mom's new work schedule conflicted with the orientation program for her daughter.

The mother and her manager tried to switch schedules with other employees but they were not able to work it out. What should the leader do?

One more. A man approached his manager, "I know that our policy requires a three-week notice prior to taking our vacation. But I need to move my mother to an assisted-living facility and I've already bought a discount (nonrefundable) airline ticket for next week."

Approve the vacation request or enforce the policy?

I once heard a boss praise a staff member, "You've done an outstanding job in blending the new programs with our current system."

The beaming employee casually reported, "I'm proud of the results. I've sweated bullets evenings and weekends over this project. My kids will be glad to see me again."

With a surprised expression, the manager responded, "I hope that you did not put too much stress on your family. I think our families come first, but we could not have achieved the result without you."

How to Select between Mission and Employee Needs

I offer two thoughts to help resolve these issues.

First, it is impossible to decide whether company demands or individual needs are most important.

Some individuals have more demanding personal needs than others, for example a single man with no dependents versus a single mother with two small children and an aging parent.

And some individuals are more capable of coping with their personal lives. Most employees manage their personal crises without asking their companies to bend. Others pressure the company over minor scrapes.

Two, compared to history, companies today award employees far more freedom and support than people could imagine one hundred or even fifty years ago.

Three weeks of paid vacation are common. Add ten or twelve days of paid holidays. Another couple of days as "personal days." Some also have "sick leave."

Pay is better. Benefits are far better. And many companies offer effective tools to help people with their personal lives, for example, Employee Assistance Programs, education on good health habits, personal fitness, financial advice, and on and on.

In sum, where the personal need is compelling, place it above the company's needs. Where the needs of individuals and demands of the company seem fairly equally balanced, it is important to support the company.

If the company does not survive, our personal needs will become even more pronounced.

E. Leaders Who Emphasize Relationships Often Sacrifice Mission

"I try to get along with my people," explained a leader. "If you do not support them, how can you expect them to work for you?"

Compare the statement to another leader who said, "My job is to get my people to commit themselves to our mission. I'll do whatever it takes to address the mission."

Leader-follower relations offer a paradox. Leaders who prioritize relationships, although they do not intend to, often sacrifice attention to mission. Leaders who focus on mission often earn better relationships.

Advocate for People or Advocate for People?

Ambrose was devoted to his people. When the home office made demands, he fought for his staff. "I'm the only thing that stands in the way of the hierarchy," he said. "If I don't protect my people, I don't know who will."

Ambrose acted as the guardian deflecting injustice from above. In turn, Ambrose's people were very loyal to him. An observer remarked, "They think Ambrose hung the moon."

Janice respected her staff, but she was totally devoted to serving the company's mission. She said, "I believe in serving our customers, and so long as I'm here, we are going to do it. Our customers deserve the best we have."

"I'm not callus toward my staff," Janice remarked. "I just think that my foremost priority is our customers."

Do You Substitute Forgiveness for Accountability?

One of Ambrose's marginal staff members mistakenly mishandled an order. The upset customer demanded and received a significant price adjustment.

The employee apologized, "I was in a hurry. I just misread the shipping orders."

Ambrose stood behind his employee and defied upper management's suggestion of moving the employee to a less responsible position.

Janice handled a similar incident quite differently. To one of her slower workers who received a customer complaint, Janice said, "I know you feel rotten about upsetting the customer, but if we don't get the orders right, we don't keep the customers. Because this has happened before, I want you to retake our customer service training course."

Is it Showing Respect or Earning Respect?

"I respect each and every one of my employees," said Ambrose. "They all have something to contribute. I treat them as mature adults, and I want to hear about their suggestions and concerns."

Janice had a slightly different take. "I treat each of my employees differently. Some I listen to; some I don't. Some I allow a lot of freedom; some I watch closely. If they want my trust, they have to earn it. I like employees who show up every day, do good work and help others—that's the way to earn my respect."

Is it Loyal to or Respect for?

Ambrose's employees liked him. "The best leader I've ever had," one said. "He looks out for our best interests."

An employee of Janice's said, "I wasn't so sure about her at first. She seemed pretty strong willed. But I have to admit, the performance of our group has improved markedly since she took over. I got a nice raise and a pretty good bonus this year."

Leaders like Ambrose may "take it easy" on their people or excuse performance failures to get support. Often this produces a combination of popular leader combined with disappointing performance and poor morale.

Janice demands performance. Because she gets performance, morale is usually very good. While she may not be voted "most popular," she will likely be quite respected.

Chapter 4: Hire

◆

(Every successful leader has a talented team.)

No matter how clear the vision or meaningful the mission, success requires talented employees. I believe that hiring decisions are the most important decisions leaders make.

Many organizations use time-consuming, bureaucratic hiring processes designed primarily to provide documentation for legal purposes.

I understand that you must hire legally. I think you must also hire quickly. This chapter suggests ways to shorten the selection process and offers hints for asking revealing questions during the selection interview. Once you have made a good hire, by all means you must keep the person on your team.

A. Speed up Your Selection Process and Hire Better People

Marty Carper, not his real name, was very excited. "I have an invitation to interview with an excellent company."

During the next three weeks, Marty's interview was put off three times due to delays in getting approvals.

Finally, the momentous interview day was set to begin with a 7:30 a.m. breakfast. Marty arrived at 7:15 a.m. By 8:00 a.m., the company representative was still a no show.

Marty called the office. After three referrals he received the message, "There must have been a mix-up. Come to the office. We'll start your interview process at 9:30."

Marty waved down a taxi and reported to the designated office at 9:15

a.m. The manager seemed surprised to see him, but quickly recovered and directed his secretary to set up an interview team.

During the day, Marty interviewed with six people but spent a cumulative total of three hours waiting around. At 6:00 p.m., the manager bid Marty farewell with the comment, "You have excellent credentials and you interviewed extremely well. We'll get back to you within a week."

Two weeks passed without any word. Marty called. After four referrals, he got the message, "Oh yes, you're our top prospect. We are waiting for a response from one more reference so our file will be complete. You will have an offer within a week." After 10 days, Marty took a job with another firm.

Every detail of this story is accurate. Although the company is a leader in the industry, managers complain that, "It is really hard to hire in this tight job market!"

Dr. John Sullivan, Professor of Human Resource Management at San Francisco State University believes that dinosaur-hiring practices lose a lot of good prospects.

"If you can't make a speed hire," Dr. Sullivan says, "you are destined to get candidates that no one else wants!"

Below are a few suggestions, many of which are based on Dr. Sullivan's ideas, for increasing the speed and quality of hiring.

1. Job descriptions—Do not *require* job descriptions or advertisements prior to hiring.
2. Interviews—Schedule interviews quickly. Make them short. Use a panel but plan ahead what questions will be asked. Do not require a minimum number of candidates. If you surface a good candidate, make the job offer the day of the interview.
3. Steps—Eliminate many steps in the hiring process. Reduce everything by at least 50 percent—number of interviews, approvals, and persons involved. Fix a time for each remaining step. Enforce the deadlines.
4. Team approvals—If you have this requirement, drop it. Allow one person to make the decision. This will be quicker and you will have more accountability.
5. Incentives—Pay bonuses to managers who hire well. One criterion for

receiving the bonus might be: The person must receive an above average review on the first performance review.

6. Instant hires—Make an instant hire if a key employee recommends the candidate.

7. Continuous—For high turnover or high growth areas, hire continuously. Yes, make an offer to a good prospect, even if you do not have an opening.

So you worry about rushing the process and hiring the wrong person? Just remind yourself that top prospects only stay in the market a few days. The longer you take to hire, the fewer high-octane candidates you keep in the queue.

Lose the lengthy bureaucratic multi-stage hiring process, which actually places more emphasis on avoiding mistakes than it does on hiring the best person. Become an ardent booster for hiring fast.

B. Make Your Decision Before You Conduct Interviews

The single most important thing that determines your success as a leader is the quality of your team. You may be the greatest leader since Peter the Great, but if your followers are no talents, you will need a magnifying glass to notice your achievements. It's an undeniable fact, "A leader (coach, vice president, business owner, and so on) is only as good as the people she leads."

When most people take leadership positions, the team is already in place. But over time, some of your team members will move on—people quit, retire, or change jobs. A few get fired.

Here are two suggestions for improving your team. One, consider every chance you get for adding a person to your team a golden opportunity. Relentlessly, seek the best candidates. Even if you have to work the second shift yourself, do not accept a "warm body" just to fill the position.

Two, make your hiring decision before your interview with the candidate.

Why Interviews are Poor Selection Tools

I have asked numerous managers, "Do you place a lot of emphasis on candidates' interviews."

Almost always, the answer is, "Yes."

"Why?" I ask.

Common responses are, "I want to know if I can be comfortable with them. I look them in the eye. I want to hear their responses. I read their body language. I check to see if we have good chemistry. I want to see if they've got it."

"Have you ever been fooled by a person during an interview?"

Most everyone answers, "Yes, more than once."

What can you really find out about a candidate in an interview that the candidate does not want you to know? I say, "Very little."

Today, many candidates rehearse their interviews. They search the internet for winning responses to your most insightful questions. They develop their interviewing techniques into a high art. Candidates with something to hide know that if they scorch the interview, there is less chance that you will discover their real warts.

But that is not the worst part. Some very good workers interview like they are on a "most wanted list." Their eyes dart to and fro. Sentences are incomplete. They fidget nervously. Answers are incoherent. Because they did poorly during the interview, they did not get to show their talents.

What can you really find out from an interview? You can find out how well a person can talk. You cannot determine whether they have the talent for the job and you can learn little about their ability to work with others.

Decide Before You Interview the Candidate

If you were required to make a decision before you interviewed the candidate, what would you do differently? Perhaps, you could more thoroughly check references. Require that all candidates provide references who will actually talk to you.

And, do not pay much attention to what the three references say. Rather, ask each for the names of two or three other people who know the candidate. Now you have six to nine additional references. Grill them with your favorite questions and a clear picture will usually emerge.

Also, study resumes and applications. Look at test results. Talk with everyone in your company who has had any contact with the applicant. From your research, select the best candidate and interview him with the idea that it is his job to lose. Show some enthusiasm. Proffer the job offer during the interview.

You will make better hiring decisions and you will enhance your chances of getting the most prized candidates to select your firm ahead of your competitors.

C. Improve Hiring Decisions by Asking the Right Questions of Candidates

When interviewing candidates for a job, do you...

1. Focus on open-ended questions about work experiences?
2. Look for specific, detailed answers?
3. Try to find out what the candidate enjoys doing?
4. Get information on previous work relationships?
5. Identify what they liked least in previous jobs?

The more effective responses are "yes" to all of the above.

"I try to find out if we have good chemistry," explained a manager when asked what he looked for when interviewing candidates.

Maybe the "chemistry" ploy worked for that manager, but most who hire well are a bit more scientific in their methods. They know what they are looking for and they have a plan to judge whether the candidate has the right stuff.

Know What You are Looking for

A manager, who did not have a very good record in hiring, said, "I do not always know what I'm looking for, but I recognize it when I see it."

By contrast, good interviewers know exactly what they are looking for.

Look for the technical requirements of the job. Must the employee know accounting? Finance? Computers? Sales techniques? What about writing skills? Telephone skills?

Further, most jobs also require soft skills. Must the employee work alone? With others? Is confrontation required? Teamwork? What about meticulous, detailed behaviors? Safety habits? Optimism? Skepticism? Upbeat attitude?

Look for Specific Answers to Open-Ended Questions

When interviewers identify exactly what they are looking for, they have solved half of the puzzle.

Managers should thoroughly research résumés and references of candidates prior to conducting a selection interview.

While the interview itself may be more art than science, the following suggestions help improve selection decisions.

1. Ask open-ended questions. For instance, "Describe a work-related success that you felt really good about."
2. Look for specific examples in answers. For example, "It happened last month. One of our largest accounts was unhappy about a shipment that was six days late. I called him the same day I heard of the complaint. I met with him in his office for 45 minutes. We agreed to use an updated version of our follow up system to avoid future delays. I got a $75,000 order from the customer three weeks later."
3. Ask candidates what they liked most about their previous job and what they liked least. While not 100-percent predictable, the odds are that the candidate will like and dislike similar things about your company.
4. Ask about partnerships or work relationships that they developed with other people. Listen for specific examples of cooperation, problem solving, conflict resolution, achievements, and disappointments.

If need be, follow up with probing questions to solicit more specific information. But I favor candidates that deliver specific and detail examples with little or no prompting.

Remember, what you hire is what you get. Leopards do not change their spots and abrasive, slow and mistake-prone candidates do not turn into cooperative, dynamic and efficient team players.

D. Check Ten to Twelve References Before You Make an Offer

"Given the information on his résumé, you would have thought he could leap tall buildings in a single bound," commented a manager about a recent hire. "He was poised and polished during his interviews. I personally called his references. One reference was very positive. Two references of former employers would only give me the dates of his employment with their firms."

The manager hired the employee. The employee had very good skills and was able to complete jobs quickly and accurately. However, after about four months on the job, troublesome issues bubbled to the surface. The employee lost his temper over a minor misunderstanding and yelled at another employee.

Bad habits sprung up like weeds after a spring rain. The employee reported jobs as complete when they were not. When the manager brought unfinished work back to him, the employee made excuses and blamed others. The good spirits he displayed during the first few months morphed into mood swings. Peers did not trust him. No one wanted to work with him.

The frustrated manager said, "I know the employee must have had trouble at his previous jobs. Most of the time, when I call references, they refer me to a human resources manager who says, 'Our policy is to give out only dates of employment on former employees.'"Most companies, to avoid potential misunderstandings and litigation, have a policy of not revealing information about former employees. Yet, former employees possess valuable, meaningful, first-hand information.

It's the Candidate's Responsibility to Provide Helpful References

I think reference checking can turn up insightful information about applicants. But you have to get references that will talk. In fact, the applicant should get permission from references before using their names.

When an applicant provides references, I ask, "Will these references be willing to answer detailed questions about your work experiences?"

If the applicant says, "No," or "I don't know," I ask the applicant for references who will provide information. When looking for a job, it is the applicant's responsibility to give me references that I can use. If they cannot, I consider the application to be incomplete.

How to Get Information from Ten or Twelve References

Traditionally, applicants provide three, hand-picked references. Some applicants give their references "talking points" and even rehearse them. It's little wonder that we seldom get useful information from applicant-supplied references.

You want to get better information from references? Dig deeper. Say to the applicant, "When I call your references, I will ask each of them for two or three other names of people who knew you. You don't mind if I do that do you?"

Most candidates will say, "Sure, go ahead." But if a candidate hesitates to give permission to add references to the list, an image of a serious red flag emerges in my mind.

With cooperative applicants, I have nine to twelve potential references, most of which have not been screened. Although it is tedious and time consuming, information from second-tier references is much more revealing. The candidate did not get a chance to prepare them.

If after talking to the second-tier references, I am still confused; I may ask the second-tier people for additional names.

The purpose for questioning references is to find out more information about the applicant's strengths and weaknesses. Consider questions such as:

1. What did the employee seem to enjoy about working there?
2. What did the employee seem to dislike about the company? Management? The job?
3. Give me an example of how the employee worked successfully with others.
4. Give me an example of when the employee was not so successful working with others.

The process is tedious and time consuming, but getting the right people on the bus is critical to your success. Reference checking is no place to take short cuts.

E. Use Probationary Period as Your Final Hiring Step

Stephen, a newly hired employee was nearing the end of his probationary period. Robin, Stephen's supervisor, reflected briefly on Stephen's performance, and without too much thought, recommended that Stephen move to regular status.

Robin did note that Stephen's performance presented some concerns. He took a little too long to finish some jobs and he let a few mistakes go through.

Robin noted these concerns and added, "Has the ability to improve."

"Frankly, I was pretty busy and did not think too much about my recommendation," admitted Robin. "I think most of us consider the probationary assignment a formality. We almost always recommend 'regular status' for our new employees."

Three years later, Stephen remained with the company, but he was not setting performance records. His performance reviews still showed problems with missed deadlines and accuracy.

Further, Stephen's pay increases had been minimal and other employees had tabbed him as a complainer.

Unfortunately, too many managers are lax when deciding whether to remove a person from probation to regular status.

Set Performance Standards High During Probation

Most organizations place new hires on a three- to six-month probationary period. This is intended to be a final check. Typically, the company policy says that the employee can be "let go" at anytime during this period and without cause. The concept is a sound one.

Management can determine, under actual working conditions, if the employee is a good fit. The employee gets to see if the company is what he/she expected.

I believe managers need to take the probationary period more seriously. I view it as the final hurdle in the hiring process. Set the standard high.

Few employees significantly improve on weaknesses that show up during their probationary assignments. Most actually get worse.

Many employees that turn out to be problems offered clues to their future during their probationary periods. Learn to read the signs.

1. Attendance. Does the employee have perfect attendance and get to work on time. Be wary of employees who miss work or show up late during probationary periods.
2. Mistakes. Is the employee's work accurate? Does he/she learn tasks and processes quickly? Employees who take too long to learn their jobs or repeat the same mistakes are sending up red flags.
3. Speed. At what pace does the employee work? Is the work completed on time? Does the employee move smoothly and quickly from one task to another? Do others complain that the new employee does not get things done on time?

   Just as plow horses do not develop into racehorses, plodding workers do not evolve into speed merchants.

4. Cooperation. Do your seasoned, high-performers complain about the new employee? Does he get along? Get into arguments? Make excuses? Blame others?

I think managers should use the probationary period to subject the employee to as many tough working conditions as possible. Above all, do not "protect" the employee from the tough parts of the job.

If, at some time, the new employee will have to work with a cranky veteran from another department, see that the employee has this experience early.

If some parts of the job are high pressure, introduce these parts at the beginning. If some tasks face quick timelines, challenge the new person to meet them.

Good employees will rise to the challenge. Employees who do not have the talent to do the job will reveal themselves. It is much more fair and dignified to release an employee during a probationary assignment than face a failed performance several years later.

Remember, it is not the employees whom you let go that make your life miserable.

F. Use Proven Techniques to Keep Good Employees

"One of my best customers has just hired one of my best employees," complained an owner. "And this is not the first time it's happened." What is a person to do or not do?

Do NOT...
- Match offers from competing companies. You do not have enough money and you would seriously disrupt salary balances among your employees.
- Go overboard with recognition programs and social events. These activities are OK, but they will not keep good people from leaving.
- Beg the employee to stay.
- Criticize the company who hired the employee. Such efforts are in vain.
- Make promises you cannot keep.
- Hire jerks with bad attitudes.

    People often get more money when they leave, but the money (unless it is a lot more) is usually not the major reason for leaving. Research tells us that employees leave when...

- their values are very different from the owner's values,
- things do not work out the way they were promised during recruiting,
- they do not like the work itself,
- they do not like the people they work with,
- they are not allowed to assume responsibility, and
- they see no opportunities for growth and promotions.

To keep good employees, begin by recruiting well. Take the time to screen people and make sure that they understand what you will expect from them.

Communicate! Keep people informed — especially key employees — of what is likely to happen. Better yet, solicit their ideas when you are trying to decide what to do.

Let employees make decisions. Support and encourage employees who make occasional mistakes. Celebrate the successes.

Periodically, show employees how they have grown with the company. If we are not reminded occasionally, we forget. Tell them what you hope for them in the future. Be realistic.

More specifically, apply the following suggestions for keeping good people.

1. Hire people with good attitudes.
2. Explain carefully what you expect of them.
3. Give good performers a lot of responsibility.
4. Support good employees when they make an occasional mistake.
5. Provide as much financial reward as you can.
6. Promote employees as quickly as you can.
7. Fire people with bad attitudes.
8. Invest in training and development.
9. Communicate everything.
10. Remain enthusiastic.

G. Five Things You Can Do to Keep Good People

"I want you to plan on a 20-percent increase in business for next year," commented a CEO to a division manager.

"We'll have no trouble getting that," responded the division manager.

"I mean I don't want you to *exceed* 20 percent," said the CEO. "We can't get enough staff to handle more than that."

Currently, the most common lament of small and mid-sized business owners is, "The big companies are hiring all of our good people." Leaders in big companies say, "The greatest limit to our growth is a shortage of skilled labor."

Skill shortage is the yang in the *ying* of any serious hiring strategy. Would you believe, though, even when there are seemingly unlimited opportunities for employees to scamper to a higher ground, some companies still retain their top performers. And here is how they do it.

One, get rid of your current losers. I hear people say, "We're hiring warm bodies." "All we can get are bottom feeders." One manager reported, "We're actually hiring criminals."

Do you wonder why it is hard to keep good people? Who wants to work in the cesspools created by unsavory hiring practices? Yes, even when you are short of people, lose the unproductive, bad attitudes from your staff and do it now!

Two, cut your employees in on the action. Let them benefit directly from the growth and success of your company. The best way to do that is to grant them bonuses linked to company performance. Many stock ownership plans work well, also.

Bonus plans come with a lot of potholes, so find an expert to help you. Some guidelines for an effective bonus are: (1) Keep it simple. (2) Make sure the bonuses are triggered by key company performance measures. (3) Grant bonuses quarterly. (4) Educate people so that they understand how the payoffs work.

One more thing, bonus plans can cause a lot of heartburn during economic downturns; and some of us have lived long enough to recall that economies do cycle. No matter how much you communicate otherwise, many employees believe that current success is everlasting.

If, in the future, employees consistently miss the bonus-triggering targets, some will think that management has given them an unfair pay cut, as exemplified by the expression, "I'm working harder now than I did during the good times!"

Three, promote from within. (We hire too many managers from outside anyway. Outside candidates have an unfair advantage—they get to prepare their own résumés.). If you promote from within, new managers already understand your culture; and it is an inspiring incentive for keeping good people.

I understand that it may be occasionally necessary to bring in a manager to add special skill or knowledge to your operation.

Four, tell employees everything. Ability to understand the overall operation is a distinct advantage for mid-sized companies. Communicate mission, vision, strategies, policy changes, financial information, customer data, hopes and fears.

It is very hard for 100,000-employee companies, because of their sheer size, to match mid-sized companies in creating "intimacy and family feelings" even when they work at it.

Five, you must invest in training and development. A manager actually reported, "We have quit investing so much in training our people. When we get people certified, they leave for better jobs."

OK, do I understand correctly, this company is going to beat its competition by hiring people and then not developing them? I do not think so! An old rule applies—training is expensive, either in direct training costs or in lost opportunities due to lack of preparation.

Of course, another option is to wait until the next downturn, whenever that may be. (Hopefully, you will have a long wait.) Then skilled people will be plentiful again.

Chapter 5: Objectives

(While processes are important, leaders focus on outcomes.)

While vision and mission provide the big picture, monthly, quarterly and annual objectives make up short-term targets.

Objectives should be specific and tangible—something you can put a number on. The better leaders discuss objectives so often that staff members can recite them in their sleep. The more meaningful objectives are the ones that determine success or failure for the organization. How we do things is important. The outcomes we strive to achieve are even more important.

A. Set Specific Objectives and Discuss Them Periodically

"What is your number one purpose?" I asked employees in a book distributing company.

"Customer service," came back the reply.

"What does customer service mean to you?" I asked.

"Customer service means that we accurately place materials in return shipment, within 24 hours after receiving an order."

"How well are you doing?"

"Last quarter we got 96 percent of the orders shipped within 24 hours with no mistakes. Next quarter we're trying for 98 percent."

Every manager on the planet knows that it is important to set objectives. Still, an alarming number of managers get caught in slow traffic when trying to motivate with objectives. Consider the following guidelines.

Make Sure Objectives are Challenging and Specific

Objectives should be hard but not impossible. Some managers believe that if you ask people to do the impossible you will get their best. Reality does not support this.

If you demand that your people jump ten feet, you will get guffaws. Ask for one foot, you will get one foot—they can already do that. Implore people to jump four feet and they will likely give you a worthy effort.

People need to believe that they have at least a 75 to 80 percent chance of achieving the results. Before staff commits to chasing high-flying objectives, managers must believe they can likely attain them.

Specific objectives are ones that you can measure—to two decimal places. Avoid objectives such as "improve morale" and "build teamwork." Sure, these are important. They are not, however, why investors spend hundreds of thousands of dollars each year to support your department.

Report Progress toward Objectives at Regular Meetings

Hold meetings at specific intervals—weekly, monthly, or quarterly —for the specific purpose of reporting progress toward objectives.

Start and end the meetings on time. You may place other items on the agenda, but put objectives first.

Encourage Discussion on How to Reach Objectives

The most intense and creative discussions occur when a department is not meeting its objectives.

For instance, "We've had a lot of trouble with our key vendor." "There is a hiring freeze and we are short on staff." "A major competitor has just moved in." "The weather has been a problem." "We need six new computers." "We did not anticipate the Russian Ruble going south on us."

When a person begins a response with an excuse, stop the person and say, "We know there are good reasons why the objective was not met. Let's spend our time talking about what corrections we should make so that we can catch up during the next period."

Meetings must not be allowed to turn into trash-littered recitations of excuses.

Show Graphs and Charts of Actual Results

In my experiences, only about 18 percent of departments use visual charts and graphs to report feedback on objectives. On average, these departments clearly outperform departments that do not report feedback in visual form.

Where staff may resist a manager's interpretation of lack of progress, they will readily accept evidence projected onto a screen in the form of line and bar charts. Visual feedback takes on a "scoreboard" aura. People are more willing to make adjustments if they have a poor "score."

The book distributing company, identified in the opening example, was very successful. In part, management achieved high performance because of the way they handled objectives.

B. Be Sure to Set the Right Objectives

I define "objectives" as end results; what the department is trying to attain. Objectives are the same as "outcomes."

Goals are more long-term and they can be more general than objectives. Goals do not help very much, though, unless we derive from them specific objectives.

Over the years, I have asked hundreds of managers and employees, "What are your top three objectives?"

Unfortunately, I often get responses such as: "Improve morale." "Teamwork." "Communication." "Add two staff members." "Purchase five personal computers." "Get everyone trained." "Get the new system installed." "Update our phone system."

While these issues may be very important, they do not meet my definition of "objectives" because they are not end results. They also are not outcomes.

Morale, teamwork, and additional staff members may be important. So important, in fact, that if you do not achieve them, you may flop as a manager. But they are not outcomes.

Concentrate Your Efforts on Objectives that Determine Success

Objectives should represent outcomes, that is, what the department was created to produce. Few departments were created to produce morale or teamwork or two new staff members.

Rather, the purpose of organizing and staffing departments is to produce something. The production may be reports, services to other departments, information, analyses, responses to customers as well as products or services to ultimate consumers. Thus, the key objectives should be the fulfillment of these purposes.

Examples of Objectives that are Likely to be Meaningful

For instance, the following are more likely to be meaningful objectives: "To produce accurate financial reports by the fifth day of the month." "To accurately conduct an average of 1,000 lab tests a week." "To ship 95 percent of our orders within 24 hours." "To produce 300 tons of paperboard a day."

To identify appropriate objectives, answer the question, "Why was the department created?" Then put measures on the answer. Key objectives can be stated in terms of quantity, quality and cost, as in, "We need to deliver twelve monthly reports by the fifth day of the month with no mistakes and stay within our budget."

Further, all department members should know exactly what the two or three key objectives are. And the department manager and his superior should be in complete agreement on the key objectives.

It seems to me that ineffective managers are more likely to stress morale and communication issues when they fail to meet their objectives. This can be a costly mistake.

Sometimes it may be necessary to increase stress and actually dampen morale to achieve the objectives. For instance, cost cutting, increased services to customers, reduced staff and the like are not fun and they are not morale building. Yet, managers may sometimes have to do these things to survive and accomplish their objectives.

Managers who focus on significant departmental outcomes are more likely to be effective. Why? Because they do what the department was created to do.

C. Avoid Confusing the Means with the Ends

"What are your three most important objectives?" I asked a manager.

"My most important objectives," he responded, "are to improve attitudes, communication and morale."

"Why do you want to improve in these areas?"

"Because our attitudes are bad. We need to improve our attitudes."

"Why do you want to improve attitudes?"

"We're having a lot of trouble with performance, so we need to improve attitudes."

"Now, let me see if I understand. Your performance is bad so you want to improve attitudes?"

"Yes, that's right!"

"If your performance is bad, why don't you make improved performance your number one objective?"

"First, we need to improve communication and morale."

This manager, I think, engaged in the too-common practice of confusing means and ends.

"Means" are Processes; "Ends" are Results

"Means" are processes that leaders use to get results. "Ends" are the results (objectives) that leaders seek.

Examples of "ends" include: increased sales by 10 percent; reduced scrap to no more than 1 percent; higher than 98 percent on-time shipments, increased return on investment by 15 percent; reduced costs by 5 percent; and so on.

Examples of "means" include: improved communication, more training, installed a software upgrade, increased teamwork, more efficient meetings, and the like.

Too frequently, managers concentrate more on the processes (the means) than they do the objectives (the ends).

Ensure that You Focus on the "Ends"

I understand that improved communications, teamwork, and morale are good things. But they are not why investors put their dollars into a company.

To test this statement, assume that your output drops 20 percent. Report to your boss, "Yes, our output is down, but we have the highest morale of any division in the company."

If your output is down 20 percent, I do not think you will be receiving a company jacket at your annual awards meeting—not even if your morale soars higher than the Empire State Building.

To managers, who worry that morale needs improving, I have asked, "Would you trade another 10 percent decline in morale if you could increase your output by 20 percent?"

Most respondents answer, "Yes, but I don't see how you can do that."

My concern with such a response is that it shows an incorrect focus for the leader. Profits! Output! Performance! Quality! Cost control! The end results! These should be the focus of leaders.

Processes Are Important

Yes, processes—communication, teamwork, methods, and procedures—are very important.

So is oxygen and water important to all leaving creatures. But few of us identify our life's purpose as: obtain oxygen or increase our water supply. Oxygen and water are simply necessary to sustain life while we pursue meaningful purposes.

It may be necessary to analyze and change processes to increase performance. But we should always remember that we invest money and time in teamwork only because this increases the odds of being profitable—or reaching other valued objectives.

Some failed leaders devote budget, time, and effort to create beautiful processes. Media may even publicize such beautiful processes. Other industry leaders express envy. Prestigious groups honor the prized processes with national awards.

Still, if profits go south on a rapid transit, the leader has failed.

There are usually many processes and methods that can lead to success. Effective leaders do emphasize "means." But when a process fights with an objective, successful attainment of the end results always takes a higher priority.

Achievement of an ugly outcome is better than the success of a pretty process.

D. Use Metrics to Measure Progress toward Objectives

"What is your most important priority for the next six months?" I asked a group of managers.

"Build quality products," said one.

"What does your department do?" I asked.

"We make and ship parts to manufacturers—our customers."

"And building a quality product is your highest priority?"

"Yes. Our second priority is to ship the product on time."

"In fact, our company would come upon some pretty hard times if we failed to get quality product to our customer on time."

Get Your Highest Priority Right

Managers and employees continuously surprise me by what they report as their highest priorities at work.

All activities of a department are no doubt important. But departments exist to produce or create output. It is this output that is always the highest priority.

I think the development and use of metrics (key performance measures) help managers and employees focus their efforts.

Metrics are Tangible Measures of Activities and Outputs

Metrics are numbers that sum up important activities and outputs. All departments, in my opinion, should have metrics that measure quality and quantity.

Managers should—and most do—have access to many measures. But I think it is important to select measures of quality and quantity as the most critical. This allows you to keep a laser focus and a magnified intensity on what you need to do.

Examples of Quality Measures

Quality measures tell us how well we do what we do.

Many organizations like universities, hospitals, and accounting firms deliver very important, albeit intangible, services. How do you measure the quality of education or health care, for example?

For education, measures may be the number of graduates employed after graduation or average starting salaries. For health care, a quality measure could be average recovery rates or percent of correct diagnoses.

Quality measures for sales could be repeat customers or the number of complaints. For parts manufacturers, metrics might include rework or rejects. The number of mistakes, satisfaction ratings from users, could be measures of the quality of financial reports.

Examples of Quantity Measures

Volume of output is important to all departments. One metric should be a simple index of the amount of product or service that a department produces.

A quantity measure of a sales department may be total units sold, net sales, or sales per person. Quantity measures of shipping departments could be percentage of on-time deliveries, or pounds per person shipped, or number of units shipped per day.

Output measures for universities might be number of persons graduated per year, number of credit hours taught or students enrolled. For hospitals, an important metric might be room occupancy rates, admissions, or number of procedures performed. The numbers of payables processed or receivables collected are quantity measures of financial operations.

For creative groups, like design, why not measure the number of hours to complete the task? Or actual hours compared to budgeted hours?

The important aspect of metrics is to generate and use accurate and reliable measures of what you are producing and how good it is.

E. Focus Measures on Outcomes; Not on the Means

"Measure." "Measure." "Measure." That is what many managers recommend for improving performance.

And it is true. Managers who are top ten performers typically place a lot of emphasis on measurements.

All Measurements Are Not Equal

It sounds simple to recommend that managers pay attention to measurements. Most organizations regularly measure and report on hundreds of behaviors. It is impractical to focus on all of them.

As one manager commented, "Too many managers fail because they highlight the wrong measures."

Most organizations keep track of how well employees are complying with policies, for instance attendance. I expect that 99 percent of all organizations can report their average attendance and whether attendance in any given month is up or down.

Organizations also require employees to measure how well they follow company procedures. Managers enforce documentation to ensure that procedures are followed when purchasing supplies, hiring employees, approving vacations, allowing overtime, requesting approval for travel, conducting performance reviews, and disciplinary actions.

We place a lot of importance on following policies and procedures, some of which are quite tedious and detailed. Then we hire huge staffs to ensure that we measure how well we enforce these actions.

Consider parking. Many organizations have numerous parking rules. They draw different colored lines in parking areas, identify lots with different letters, and require employees to place stickers on their vehicles. To measure for compliance, they hire huge staffs to observe and count the percentage of violations.

One manager proudly reported to me measures on the number of tickets issued. He even had them broken into categories such as: "parking in unassigned spaces," "out-of-date stickers," "stickers improperly displayed," "number of cars towed," and "violations for parking in 'handicapped spaces.'"

Emphasize the Data that Measure Important Outcomes

I like data. I do not suggest that we quit measuring any work behaviors. Statistics on such things as the number of candidates applying for a particular job this year as compared to five years ago can help us make better decisions.

The problem is that we find ourselves swimming in a sea of data with little effort to prioritize its importance.

I just believe that there are three measures in any given job that are much more important than all of the other statistics. I am talking about measures of quantity, quality, and costs.

Quantity measures include how much of something we have made or how many people we have served. Total sales, units shipped, people served, reports delivered, projects completed, and tonnage shipped are examples.

Quality measures indicate how well we did what we did. Examples include: defects, customer complaints, returns, mistakes, errors, warranty issues, and scrape rate.

Costs identify how many dollars we have spent on labor, materials, supplies and overhead to produce the product or deliver the service, for instance: labor unit costs, materials costs, and overhead allocated.

Sure, managers can tell you exactly how many days each of their employees have been late or absent. But can they tell you how many units of product or service each employee has produced?

Effective managers look at all of the numbers. But they look the longest and hardest at the numbers that determine their success.

Chapter 6: Empower

(Most leaders talk about empowerment; few walk the walk.)

What is the difference between delegation and empowerment? Not much, really. Delegation is short for delegation of authority. Authority is the organizational right to make decisions. When leaders delegate authority, they allow their subordinates the right to make decisions.

Leaders who refuse to delegate, ask subordinates to refer all important, and most routine, decisions to them. Subordinates who do not have authority often use a phrase similar to, "I'll have to run this by my boss."

When leaders empower subordinates, they encourage subordinates to make decisions without checking. I think the word "empowerment" is simply the more modern term for "authority delegation."

More than 60 percent of workshop participants say they have trouble with authority delegation. As one honest manager stated, "Frankly, it's just hard for me to let go." This is understandable. Most leaders get promoted because they make good decisions. Naturally, it is hard for many, especially newly-promoted leaders to sufficiently trust staff members to make decisions.

A. Real Leaders Know What Decisions They Should Make and What Decisions Their Subordinates Should Make

"How many of you are currently in supervisory or management positions?" I asked about two hundred convention participants.

Eighty-five percent of the audience raised their hands.

"How many of you are expected to sometimes roll up your sleeves, get your hands on the work and do some of the work yourself?" was my follow-up question.

Almost all of the eighty-five percent raised their hands again.

Then I asked, "How many of you often cannot tell the difference between what it is that you should be doing and what it is that your subordinates should be doing?"

And again, almost all of the eighty-five percent raised their hands.

First-line and mid-level managers, it appears to me, face two huge challenges on how to allocate their efforts. One, what should they do and what should they require their subordinates to do? Two, how do you get subordinates to do things that you have been doing.

Leaders Spend More on Goals, Objectives, and Improvements

When first promoted into a management job, many people continue to do a lot of what they were doing before they became managers. Effective managers decide early on what they should and should not do.

I have observed that the more effective managers spend a lot of time doing things like: talking about goals and objectives, measuring progress, developing budgets, monitoring spending, improving policies and procedures, communicating, inspiring, resolving conflicts, checking the work of others, praising staff, improving services, cutting costs, improving quality, asking questions, and suggesting new ways.

In general, managers should not do what their staff members are hired to do, for example: routine and repetitive tasks, building, fixing or repairing products or services, calculating, inputting data, filling out reports, finishing an employee's task, correcting other's mistakes, completing undone work, sweeping the floors or turning out the lights.

How to Effectively Delegate Authority to Staff

To the convention group, I asked, "Are you doing anything that others in your group can and should be doing?"

Almost all raised their hands. Most of us, if we were honest with ourselves, would answer "yes" to that question.

To get your employees to do what they should be doing, but what you have been doing for them, try the following:

1. Make a list of things that you are currently doing that employees really should be doing.
2. Group the activities into logical groups, for example, compiling, report preparation, ordering; and give them a name.
3. Identify specific persons to do the items.
4. Approach the selected persons with confidence and say, "Beginning Wednesday, I want you to be responsible for (name the group of activities)." Politely, answer questions and offer suggestions when appropriate.
5. Try to stay away from the employee on Wednesday—not because you wish to avoid the person but if you are nearby, you will likely be a nuisance and the employee's stress level will approach meltdown.
6. Find something in the new assignment, no matter how hard you have to look, that the employee is doing well and praise her for it.
7. Most important, refuse to do the work that you have assigned to the employee. This is the real test. If the employee does not do the work properly, the work does not get done. If you are not willing to take this chance, you will very soon be doing the work yourself.

If employees are to "own their new tasks," they must perceive that if they do not do the work, it does not get done. Most employees, with the right support, will readily assume more responsibility.

B. Empowerment is Much More than Merely Assigning Tasks

Management professors have discussed empowerment (and formerly, authority delegation) for longer than citizens have discussed problems in the public school systems.

Scholars have argued the benefits of empowerment. Practitioners have struggled with how to empower. Consultants have prescribed fail-safe methods for turning chronic whining employees into responsibility seekers.

A few years ago, some started calling delegation "empowerment" in an effort to reenergize delegation efforts. Still, most leaders struggle with the concept. Many misunderstand it.

To Empower is to Encourage Subordinates to Make Decisions

If you look at it mechanically, empowerment involves three steps. One, assign a task to a subordinate. Two, give the subordinate the right to make decisions. Three, check the results.

The operative step is number two, "Give the subordinate the right to make decisions necessary to complete the assignment."

Example of a Task Assignment

A manager trained one of his subordinates in a customer service function. He went into great detail to explain the store's procedures for taking returned merchandise.

The procedure included a six-step method. The manager emphasized, "If you think there is a need for deviation from any of this procedure, you must get my approval."

During the first few days of the new assignment, the manager checked several times to see if the employee had any questions; and the employee called the manager a half a dozen times with questions.

This is not empowerment. Rather it is task assignment. The manager made all of the decisions. The employee robotically carried out the steps of the assignment.

Example of Empowerment

A manager of a delivery company trained an employee on taking items for delivery.

During the training, the manager emphasized, "Our number one priority is to get items to the proper destination at the time we promise with no damage. Our goal is 98 percent on time and we've got to make money doing it."

The manager added, "So long as it is legal and ethical, do what you need to do to accomplish the result."

This example is true empowerment because the manager encouraged the employee to make decisions rather than blindly follow prescribed procedure.

Effective Empowerment Overcomes Two Challenges

No matter how much you stress making decisions, employees will be tempted to call you on their cell phones with questions about how to handle something. Or, employees will ask if it is OK to do this or not do that.

Ineffective leaders provide specific and detailed answers to employees who experience problems. Employees feel safe in this environment. As an employee reported, "If I use my boss's solution and it does not work, then it was not my fault."

Effective responses include: "How are you going to handle that problem?" Or, "Do you think you should do it or not?"

Put the decision back to the employee. Nurture employees to act on their own.

A second challenge occurs when employees make mistakes, which they surely will do. It is important to avoid overreacting. Managers who overreact to occasional mistakes cause employees to avoid seeing (or reporting) problems.

As an employee reported, "My manager told me to take care of a situation. Afterwards, he told me he did not like my solution. The next time that problem came up, I made sure that I was busy with something else."

When good employees make occasional mistakes, support them. You will encourage employees to take more initiative and you will get better results.

Chapter 7: Communicate

◆

(It is impossible for poor communicators to be great leaders.)

When President Abraham Lincoln was assassinated, it was several weeks before the citizens of England heard about it. If, heaven forbid, a public person were to be assassinated today, it would take seconds for images of the catastrophe to spread around the world.

Today, there is so much information communicated to so many people, it is easy to become overloaded and confused. Organizations face the same dilemma. Both employees and managers want to know everything and they want to know it immediately.

The act of communication is a complex event. When leaders must communicate with hundreds, even thousands, of people of many backgrounds, cultures and countries; it is a miracle that we understand each other as well as we do.

A. The Best Way to Improve Communication is to Improve Relationships

Answer "true" or "false" to each of the following:
Most employees…

1. Believe that management should communicate better.
2. Think that management does not listen well enough.
3. Say that the grapevine is their greatest source of information.
4. Believe that they are not "in the loop" regarding communication.
5. Think that management often withholds key information.

6. Say that they prefer to get their information directly from their supervisors.

7. Believe that a lot of time in meetings is wasted.

My research suggests that "true" is the correct answer for all of these statements.

Most Managers Try to Communicate Well

I believe that the vast majority of all managers hold communication in the same high regard as they do their golf handicap.

Managers literally bombard employees with information. They hold meetings, publish newsletters, install television monitors, crank out emails, send updating voice messages, post data on countless bulletin boards, and encourage open door policies.

Yet, every few years, some professor will conduct still another survey and report, "Guess what?" "Employees say their managers need to improve communication."

Managers react to the findings with a renewed determination. They discuss communication in their executive retreats; promise to dedicate even more time to it, and demand that staff deliver data by the wheelbarrow load.

Employees Want to Know Everything Now

Employees are grateful to get information and they especially like to get it fast.

"I remember," recalls a long-time senior manager, "when someone in most every meeting would interject the phrase, 'Let's keep this information in this room.'"

Now the likely phrase is, "Let's make sure that we keep our employees informed about these discussions."

I am absolutely certain that managers today are reporting more things more quickly than ever before.

But in a short time, people adjust to the "new speed" and the "new openness." Now, they want it just a little quicker.

I recently overheard an insightful manager comment, "I don't think my people will be happy with our communication until they know all that I know at exactly the moment that I know it."

I believe he summed up the dilemma correctly.

Improve Communications by Improving Relationships

Additional information is not the answer! Getting information out faster is not the answer! Even if we communicated at warp speed, we would not meet everyone's expectations. The answer to better communication, I believe, is improved personal relationships.

I work in an institution with more than fifteen hundred employees. Dr. Donald Beggs, the President of the University, has built genuine, personal relationships with hundreds of the University's employees.

When President Beggs stops me on campus and sincerely asks how my bird dogs are doing, I can assure you that I do not criticize him for lack of communication.

Leaders who do better at communication take sincere special interests in their people. They know their employees' passions, their family lives, their worries, and their joys. And they know this without prying.

Good communicators are, of course, honest. But they are also warm, friendly, open and supportive. Employees cherish personal relationships with these leaders.

To communicate well, managers really need for their employees to "cut them a little slack," to trust them more, to avoid second-guessing and speculating, and to maintain confidence when clouds darken.

You see, good communication is more than accurately sending and receiving facts. It is about trust, support and absence of speculation. This only occurs when leaders personalize their relationships in unique and meaningful ways.

B. What Should You Communicate When You are Unsure about What to Communicate?

I think I must be missing something.

I have asked hundreds of managers, "What are the characteristics of good communication between managers and employees?"

Unlike discussions on such topics as what political party has the high ground, most people agree that good communication is honest, open, trustworthy, complete, timely, and responsive. Good communicators also receive (spell that "listens") information well.

Managers agree. Employees agree. Experts agree. This is not one of the great mysteries of the universe.

Yet, actual practices by too many managers are not consistent with what they describe as good communication.

Managers Debate When to Communicate a Work Schedule Change

Take a case in point. Managers, in their regular weekly meeting, were very close to an agreement on changes in work schedules of a few of their personnel. The change was going to negatively impact one employee in particular because the change would require him to work two Sundays out of every month.

"I know he will not like working on Sunday," explained one of the managers. "I've heard him say that if he had to work Sundays, he would probably quit."

"I don't think he will quit," another manager said, "but you are right. He will not like the change."

From a third manager, "There is still a probability; admittedly it is slight, that we will not actually make these changes. At any rate, it will be at least two more months before anything is final. Let's hold off on communicating our decision until a couple of days before the change."

All seven managers in the meeting quickly agreed. "Good idea." said one. "There is no need creating two months of anxiety for the employee."

"And we won't have to listen to the griping for two months."

"There is a chance that we will not even make the change."

Somewhat smugly, the group agreed that they had solved their problem. They all committed to remaining silent on the matter until they had to tell the employee about the change.

I had a chance to discuss this situation with these managers. In previous discussions on communications, they had described good communication in the terms of open, honest and timely.

I asked the managers, "Was your decision not to tell the employee about the change open? Was it timely? Trustworthy? Complete? Honest?"

Every manager in the group sat slack-jawed and silent. Why? Because the answers to my questions were, "No," "No," "No," "No," and "No."

"We just thought we were looking out for the best interests of the employee," one manager meekly offered.

"If you were the employee in question," I asked, "when would you like to be told?"

All admitted that they would want to be told now, not two months from now. And all said that they sure would not want to hear about it through the grapevine—which is a very real possibility.

All of these managers were well meaning and believed that they were very considerate of their employees.

I don't get it! Why is there such a disconnect between beliefs and actions of good managers? I do not know the answer to this question.

When in Doubt, Shout it Out

I do offer simple guidelines for what and when to communicate to employees.

One, if you are sure that the information should not be communicated, do not communicate it.

Two, if you are sure the information should be communicated, do communicate it.

Three, if you are unsure about whether and when you should communicate information, by all means tell the employees and tell them now. You will have far fewer problems.

C. Improve Listening by Paraphrasing What You Heard

Respond "yes" or "no" to the following:

1. Do you frequently use the phrase, "We disagree," when someone says something that you disagree with?
2. Do you often paraphrase another's statements when you disagree?
3. Do you resist the strong urge to correct others' opinions when you think they are wrong?
4. Do you avoid trying to prove the other person wrong when he/she says you are not listening?

The answer of effective listeners to all questions is "yes."

Has anyone ever said to you, "You don't listen"?

Almost without exception, people have made this statement to us. When someone tells you that you are not listening, what is your response?

If you are typical, you say something like, "I am listening." Or, you report facts and words that the person just said to prove that indeed you were listening.

Neither of these responses suggests that we are good listeners.

Effective Listening is the First Step in Upward Communication

The first step in getting what employees are thinking is effective listening. Most of us do not do this very well. Oh, we get the facts. If someone tells us that customers are upset because we did not deliver what they bought, we get that.

And we get the facts when an employee disagrees with a performance appraisal, for example, "I don't know why I got a 'needs to improve' on my quality of work rating. I think my quality is just as good as the others."

The problem is that we get only the facts. An employee who is disgruntled about a review is likely experiencing concern, angry, worry and perhaps insecurities. We do not usually get this.

A typical supervisor would immediately offer a clear explanation to a dissatisfied employee, for example, "You are doing OK but you make too many mistakes. Let me explain why I rated you as I did."

The supervisor and employee will likely continue back and forth for a while. After the meeting, the employee comments to a friend, "My supervisor did not hear a thing I said."

This is befuddling to a supervisor. "I know the employee was upset. I explained it as clearly as I could. Why does he think I did not listen?"

Listening is about hearing, not talking; receiving, not explaining; understanding, not clarifying. Rather than explain or clarify, the supervisor could say something like, "I understand you disagree with my rating. You think I should have rated you higher?"

This is an example of an "understanding response." It is more likely to reduce tensions in the conversation. The employee might say, "Yes, I do think you rated me too low…"

The supervisor might probe, "Can you give me some examples of your recent work that we might talk about?"

By letting the employee know you are listening and by asking for additional information, you are not implying that you agree. You are simply engaging in the hard work of listening.

At some point in the conversation, it may be necessary for the supervisor to offer an explanation, preferably with examples, of why he thought the employee needed to improve.

If there is still disagreement, and there might very well be, the supervisor can conclude the conversation with, "I understand your point, but on this we just disagree."

Such an approach improves the odds of the employee commenting to friends, "I still disagree with the boss, but at least he will listen to you."

D. Learn to Assert Yourself Even in Risky Situations

During a staff meeting of five employees and a manager, the manager angrily said to an employee, "I don't know what you did to the Felix Application, but you did not render all of the services they were expecting."

The manager went on to say that he received a call from a Felix representative that really embarrassed him.

Leaning toward the employee and raising his voice, the manager continued, "I want to rely on you to get things done without having to follow up on every little detail! If you are confused, tell someone so that we can get it straightened out!"

All five staff members looked as if a harsh judge had sentenced them. The staff member who had received the leader's wrath was bewildered. He was sure, though, that he did not cause the problem.

Apparently, after the initial agreements, a Felix manager called and requested changes.

The person who took the message confirmed that the changes would be made but did not tell this to all of the persons responsible for delivering the services.

The irate manager knew about the changes. Others new about the change, but the employee being hassled for upsetting the Felix people did not know about the changes.

The employee, who is the recipient of a verbal face slapping by his leader, is a conscientious and responsible worker with a good record.

The manager was relatively new to the department and probably did not know all of his personnel very well. Some also thought the new manager did not fully understand, nor follow all of the department's internal procedures.

Consider four responses that the abused employee might make.

A. "I'm not sure what happened here. I need more information to be able to give you a good response. Could you fill me in with additional details? I want to be able to resolve this and prevent it in the future."

B. "I was disappointed in the outcome too. I'm very sorry that this has happened. Believe me I will do everything I can to stay informed and to see that this does not happen again. I hope you do not hold this one against me."

C. "I think I provided what you initially requested of me. I now understand that someone from Felix requested service modifications, but no one told me about the request. Frankly, it bothers me that you assumed that I was at fault without filling me in or checking to see what I did. I do have suggestions for how to resolve this."

D. "Wait a minute! I did exactly as we agreed. The commitment was changed and you never advised me of the change. You are putting the blame on me for something your office had control over."

Although about 70 percent of workshop participants recommend the "A" solution as the best reply, I believe that "C" is the most honest, open and direct response. Thus, "C" meets more of the requirements of assertive communication.

I think the "B" response is too submissive and the "D" response is too aggressive. Some suggest that "C" is too risky. The employee could be in the boss's doghouse until the spring thaw.

I have no especial quarrel with the "A" response. It simply does not represent the truth of how most people would think and feel if they were in the situation.

I agree that honest, open and direct communication often carries risks. I submit that passive or submissive responses are also risky. The boss may think the employee is too weak for responsible assignments; peers may lose respect for the employee; the boss may continue to abuse.

Assertive communicators take the risks of being open, honest and direct about what they think and how they feel.

E. How to Communicate When You are in Different Parts of the Country

"Do your managers ever come out to visit at your location?" I asked a group of employees who worked at a site distant from the office.

"They come out about once in a 'blue moon.'"

"Is there a schedule? Do they come out quarterly? Annually?"

"No, there is no schedule. They usually come out when they think we have messed something up."

"You mean when they get a bad report? Or when sales drop? Or a customer complains?"

"Exactly. Things can go swimmingly for months and we never see them. But let us stumble and they show up out of nowhere."

A manager says, "They are so far away, I go for weeks sometimes without seeing them. I may not even know of a problem until it is too late."

There is no question, geographical distance does challenge communications. Leaders who communicate well with remote locations use a combination of media.

Researchers G. S. Ross and R. L. Daft, writing in the *Management Communication Quarterly,* have ranked communication media according to signal richness—the amount and speed of signals transmitted.

Face-to-Face. Without question, the most signal-rich means of communication is face-to-face. If at all possible, sensitive communications should occur face-to-face. From 60 to 80 percent of the signals in face-to-face communication are nonverbal—gestures, frowns, smiles, eye movements, body posture, voice tone, and the like. When we are not looking eye to eye with each other, we lose these signals.

Site visits are important and they should occur on a regular basis—not just when there is an apparent need.

Video Conferences. While not quite as communication rich as face-to-face, video conferences do a pretty good job of conveying nonverbal signals.

Speakers and cameras attached to computers make video conferencing assessable and inexpensive. If you do not have the technology, consider investing in it. If you have the technology, use it.

Telephone. The old-fashioned telephone is still an excellent communication tool. Telephones do drop out visual images, but they still include voice volume and tone. Use the telephone frequently. Call when there is no need to call. Make visits brief. Today's cell phones make this technology even more user friendly.

Voice mail. I got a voice mail recently that said, "This is so and so. Call me." I called back promptly, got the other person's voice mail, and left a message that said, "I'm returning your call." We played telephone tag several times before we finally connected.

As a minimum, when you leave a voice message, tell why you called, identify how urgent the issue is, and give some suggested times when you would be available for a call back.

If you phrase your voice messages artfully, you can address a lot of issues simply by exchanging your recordings.

Email. Personally, I like emails a lot. They are fast, convenient and allow flexibility in communications.

On the down side, they leave out all nonverbal signals. And some persons struggle with expressing themselves in writing. Also, if a person "hunts and pecks" the keyboard with two fingers at a rate of about 10 words per minute, emails are not so fast.

There are many other tools for communicating over distance, but they are not so efficient. Letters and memos (snail mail) are too slow in the age of email. Company videos are too expensive, too static and cannot change quickly enough. Websites are OK, but require constant upkeep. Written and numerical documents may be necessary for transmitting information, but they are the least media rich.

When distance is great, use a combination of means, make frequent contacts, and initiate the communication before there is a real need.

F. Use Voice Mail to Enhance, Not Impede, Communication

"I'm on the phone or away from my desk right now. Please leave a message at the beep."

Is there a more irritating communiqué? Well, maybe. What about, "Our offices are open from eight to five, Monday through Friday. Please call back during these hours or leave a message at the bleep."

Why am I turning blue? It's 10:30 a.m. on Wednesday!

Here is another one.

"If you would like information about service, press one. If you would like a copy of our brochure, press two. If you wish to talk to George, press three. If you want to talk to a real person, press zero."

Then I press zero. Guess what? "I'm on the phone or away from my desk…"

Here is a polite version of the message I would like to leave, "Does anyone work there?"

Sometimes I get a note asking me to check my voice mail. I do. The message is, "This is Nancy, please call me." That's it? Is there a subject? Question? Do I need to do anything? Are you experiencing gall bladder troubles again?

OK, so I call back, and—you guessed it—I get Nancy's voice mail.

Voice mail, thanks to the age of technology, has many potential benefits. Voice mail answers the phone twenty-four hours a day, seven days a week, eliminates costly labor, takes complex messages, and captures the tone, pace and nuisance of speech—something email cannot do.

Further, you can dial in from space at midnight on Saturday and pick up your messages.

But like any tool, voice mail has the potential for abuse. Some systems are so complex, it takes a month's supply of patience to get through all of the options; and it is easy for staff to abuse this telephone technology. For instance, I approached an office where a staff member was working. "I just called you," I said.

"Oh," came the response. "I had a lot of work to do so I put the phone on voice mail."

One frustrated manager reported. "A voice mail from a staff member explained that he was faxing some materials to me. The materials came in over the fax. I checked my email and there was a message asking if I had received the fax. A day later, I got a hard copy of the materials."

Do we really need this much redundancy?

Even with all of the technology available, people still complain that we need to improve our communication. Perhaps technology is neither the real problem nor the real answer.

Good communication requires individuals who are willing to make time to discuss things while being clear, candid and open to each other's ideas. The use of technology does not guarantee this to happen.

Since voice mail is here to stay, below are some simple guidelines for its use.

When leaving a voice message:

- Identify yourself clearly.
- Summarize the reason for your call.
- Let the person know a good time and place to reach you.

When using a voice mail system, don't:

- Leave it on when you are in the office.
- Make the recorded message too complex.
- Substitute the recording for personal contact.
- Use it to replace needed personnel.

Do you recall when busy signals were our greatest source of frustration with telephones?

G. Keep Emails Effective by Writing Brief and Grammatically Correct Messages

A president of a large company resigned because his affair with a subordinate became public. And how did others discover the liaison? Email! For months, the two parties communicated passionate love notes via email.

I certainly do not condone the executive's bad judgment, or his moral lapse for that matter. But I cannot help but think, "Why would intelligent people in high positions document their illicit relationships with email messages?" Are these the only two people on the planet who think electronic messages have the characteristics of disappearing ink? Or is this evidence to support the saying, "Love is blind."

Millions of adults use email daily. Worldwide, we send more than a trillion messages daily. I know one large company that prohibited its employees from using email because they were exchanging messages so often; the president thought it was a distraction to their work.

Personally, I like email a lot because it is quick, inexpensive and easy to store. Consider the following do's and don'ts when using email.

1. Consider messages to be public. Avoid writing anything in an email that you do not want reported in your local media. By all means, avoid writing disparaging comments about your boss in an email to a friend. Companies have the right to monitor your messages and some do it. Just assume that there is an electronic fairy somewhere that saves all email messages for eternity.

2. Check for spelling and grammar. Fortunately, we do not have to worry about penmanship. But it seems that we do lower our spelling and grammar standards in email. Proofread thoroughly before sending. At least, use spell check. Although email readers may be more tolerant of spelling and sentence structure than newspaper editors, people still judge you by what and how you write.

3. Keep messages brief. Use short words, short sentences and short paragraphs. Elaborate explanations need face-to-face contact. Avoid messages that include copies of ten previous messages. If you are going to write a "book," most of us still prefer a hard copy, or at least a Kindle version.

4. Avoid broadcasting to the multitudes. Messages are more effective when one person sends specific content to one other person. Email is still pretty effective when you send a message to a dozen close associates. Beyond some number, however, receivers lose interest. As one person commented, "If the message goes to five hundred people, the sender must not consider me to be very significant."

5. Use the subject line. When I receive a message with a subject line of "none," I do not open the message. If the subject is nonsensical or something that I do not recognize, likewise the message goes in the "delete" box. Better yet, try to get attention with the subject line. For instance, a subject line that reads, "Trip to Orlando Approved," is better than "Travel."

6. Avoid using email to transmit emotional messages. Most of the meaning in face-to-face communication is nonverbal. Email leaves out facial expressions, voice tone, and body posture. If the message is sensitive or

likely to arouse strong emotions, deliver it in person. If you are half a continent away, use a telephone.

7. Use the "forward" key sparingly. Messages that are forwarded to twenty people and then forwarded to another twenty lose impact. While an occasional "forward" to another person accompanied by a personal note is fine, mass forwarding takes on the essence of junk mail.

8. Close the loop. When someone sends you an email, let them know that you received it. If the email requests an action, tell them what you will do. If the email simply conveys a message, take three seconds to write back something; "Thanks!" "Got it." "Will respond next week." Otherwise the sender is left to wonder whether the message got to you or was gobbled up by the elusive, electronic email monster.

H. Manage Rumors by Getting in on the Office Gossip Grapevine

A memo from a mid-manager to all of her supervisors read, "The grapevine found its way to my office. I've heard that some supervisors have told their employees that they will get off work early on Thursday before the Friday holiday. If this is true, the information is wrong."

The memo went on to request, "If any of you are aware that supervisors have told their people they can leave early, please report their names to me."

The odds of a supervisor turning in the name of peer on anything are about equal to the odds of Tiger Woods missing a two-foot putt.

One supervisor did report that one of his employees had been granted a family emergency leave to care for an elder parent on the day prior to the holiday.

Another reported that she had an employee who was on sick leave.

In a follow-up memo, the manager communicated, "All supervisors reported to me that they have not told employees they can leave early or miss work on Thursday. However, I expect our unexcused absences may be slightly higher. Please monitor this and handle according to our policy."

Managers Make Mistakes when Dealing with the Grapevine

In my opinion, this manager made four classic mistakes.

One, she communicated a general message that implicitly placed all employees under a suspicious cloud.

Two, she over reacted to one piece of information. And it turned out to be a false rumor.

Three, her immediate reaction was to distrust her supervisors.

Four, she communicated in impersonal fashion (an email memo). Face-to-face communication in a meeting or informal visits would have been better.

Managers are often Unaware of Office Gossip

Company grapevines are important to employees. Some studies show that as many as 60 to 70 percent of employees hear things through the grapevine before management announces them.

Further, employees believe that information in the grapevine is actually more reliable than management communications.

Grapevine information is important to managers also. But grapevines bypass managers even when the information is common knowledge among employees.

For example, Robert abruptly resigned from his managerial position after 15 years. Eighty percent of employees had heard that he would likely resign. Only 10 percent of managers had heard the rumor.

In another case, a top executive resigned when emails to his mistress, who was also his subordinate, became public. The relationship had long been grapevine fodder for employees. Other managers were shocked to learn of the situation.

Suggestions for Assessing the Grapevine

Managers certainly need to be aware of employee grapevine issues. Informal employee discussions and rumors identify concerns that cause employee anxiety.

Grapevine talk can also give feedback to management on how well their communication is being received.

How can managers tap into the grapevine? Not be sending memos requesting information on gossip and rumor.

Develop trust by communicating specific events like changes in policy, personnel, locations, and employment levels quickly. Tell the bad news as well as the good.

Get out of the office. Visit with employees. Get to know them personally.

Listen to what they have to say. Do not argue and do not scold employees for telling you things, no matter how outlandish the rumor may sound.

Employees will tell their bosses the latest "gossip" only when they trust them.

I. Keep Management Presentations Simple, Brief and Enthusiastic

Toastmasters, a group of people who give members practice in making presentations, proclaim that a person's second greatest fear is fear of talking in front of a group. What then is our greatest fear? It's fear of dying.

The first rule of speechifying is to keep it simple. The second rule is to keep it brief. After listening to an unnecessarily dry, lengthy and academic delivery on an esoteric subject, a colleague said to me, "That guy is really brilliant. I don't have a clue of what he was trying to get across."

"I don't think he was all that smart," I replied.

"Why do you say that? Did you understand him?"

"No, that's the point. If he had been brilliant, he would have found a way to communicate his ideas so that we could understand them."

The purpose of a presentation is to communicate, not to dazzle with vocabulary.

Content is More Important than Style

To help people understand and remember, tell a story. Tie your comments together with a common theme. For instance, "I will explain the ailments of our current payroll system, take a journey through other options, and end with a solution that will increase accuracy and reduce costs."

As one wit said, "In God we trust, everyone else should bring data." Avoid general and meaningless phrases such as, "the best," "the most dependable," or "great improvements."

Such phrases are conclusions. You are simply asking the audience to agree with whatever you say. Give the audience more credit. Report the data. Allow them to come to the right conclusions. For example, "rated first in the industry," "a 98.5% on time delivery record," "20 percent improvement in accuracy in operations similar to ours."

Focus on two or three major points. You should be able to persuade people to accept your recommendation with just your top three reasons. If they do not buy it on the three most important reasons, you are surely not going to convince anyone with justifications numbered 4-15.

Be Enthusiastic if You Want to Keep Your Audience's Attention

How you tell the story is important. Show some passion. You have spent a lot of hours on the project. You may not be splitting the atom, but you have got to believe you are doing something really important.

Get excited. Raise and lower your voice. Talk fast. Flap you arms. Point your finger. Call people by name. Look at the audience. Tell a funny anecdote. Let people see your charm. Whatever you do, DON'T READ FROM THE BLANKETY-BLANK SCREEN! This I will guarantee, unless you look like Julia Roberts or Tom Cruise, the audience does not want to see your backside.

Use Stage Props to Focus Your Message

Years ago, I was on the program with a popular presenter. As we arrived at the stage, I noticed that he had one of the hotel towels in his hand.

"What are you doing with that towel?" I asked.

"I never give a talk without a stage prop," he said.

During his 15-minute talk, he raised, lowered, swung and referred to that towel a dozen times as he drove home the critical importance of customer service.

Pictures are fine. PowerPoint slides are fine so long as they contain only a few bullet points. Better yet, show appropriate cartoons, pertinent quotes, and insightful pictures. Avoid PowerPoint slides that show long lists of things. Bring a sample of something. Present a diagram, an artist's rendering. Bring a model.

When your audience leans forward, interrupts, asks questions and argues your points, relax and enjoy it. They are engaged because you are communicating.

Chapter 8: Decide

◆

(The decision not to make a decision is a decision.)

"Where would you like to go to lunch?" asked a friend.
"I don't know," was the reply.
"You decide."
"No, you decide."

You have had this conversation. If you are hungry, you may starve sitting in the driveway. "Someone make a decision and let's get out of here!"

The ability to make good decisions, I believe, is one of the talents of great leaders. I am not sure effective decision making can be taught. Some managers seem to have the knack, some do not. But one thing is sure, it is impossible for a leader to get the commitment of followers without clear, clean and confident decisions.

A. Make Decisions for the Right Reasons

Should we raise the price? Lower the price? Would Bob make a better manager? Or would Mary do the job more effectively? Should we add another product line? Drop some of our lines?

What is the best way to promote our services? Structure our organization? What should we spend on capital equipment? Which software system should we install? Have we chosen the right location? Are our objectives correct?

Whom should we hire? I wonder if it is time to terminate this employee who cannot seem to do things right? Should we buy or lease? Which bank should we solicit?

We talk a lot about what makes an effective leader. Authorities argue over styles—autocratic versus democratic, demanding versus easy, directive versus supportive, centralized versus decentralized, micromanaging versus empowering, nice versus mean.

For me, I'll take the leader who makes good decisions. No matter what the leader's style, the opportunity to win the gold comes only if the leader makes good choices.

As an acquaintance commented, "I worked for the nicest, most participating, supportive, facilitating leader you will ever meet. But we made two bad decisions—we brought out a new product that fizzled and we purchased a 'miracle' software system that cratered. Our division was sold."

Often, in my opinion, decisions are made for the wrong reasons.

If You Shy Away from Unpopular Decisions, You Often Get Bad Decisions

What is wrong with the following comments?

"I think you have a good idea for improvement, but I don't think my boss will approve it."

"I have a subordinate that I should fire, but Human Resources gets on our case when we try to terminate people."

"I think the boss's proposed organizational restructuring is a nightmare, but I'm not going to anger him by opposing it."

All of these comments suggest that the primary reason for the decisions is to avoid upsetting someone.

Too many managers, I believe, shy away from unpopular decisions even when they are justified. Further, managers have a bias toward making decisions that they think will put them in a good light with others.

It seems that avoiding upsets and currying favors weigh too heavily in decision making. Surely, it is appropriate to consider the impact of decisions on others. But when the winning reason is, "to avoid upsetting someone," the decision is usually not for the good of the company.

Not only do you get a lame decision when the intent is to avoid angering others, you actually reward persons prone to getting upset. Avoiding the disapproval of others then becomes too much of an influence in decision making.

Whether a decision is supported by all, was made to avoid bad feelings, or is good politics; these really should not be issues.

Leaders Select Choices that Serve the Company's Mission

The proper intent of decisions is to serve the organization's mission.

The concerns should be: "Will this decision advance our objectives?" "Does this give us the best chance of achieving our mission?"

I do believe in some boundaries for decisions. For instance, it is important to pass these tests: "Is the decision fair to customers, investors, and employees?" "Is the decision ethical?" "Is the decision legal?" And most important of all, "Is this decision the right thing to do?"

During the course of a year, leaders make literally thousands of decisions. Many are minor and a few are significant, but all impact the organization's viability.

I would like for my leader to be pleasant, kind, and respectful. I would also like for my leader to ask for, and seriously consider, my suggestions on things that affect me and my department.

But above all, I enjoy working in a successful organization. To achieve this, it is necessary that the leader make good decisions, no matter what his/her personal style may be.

B. Good Decisions Improve Performance, Morale, and Inner Peace

We make thousands of them, decisions I mean, every week. Most are automatic—how to handle a customer, what to put on our meeting agenda—but some are complex and puzzling.

Consider these three examples:

1. "I have a staff member who has been a good performer. He is going through personal troubles now and he is just not performing. It would be better for our company if I replaced him. I don't know if this is the best thing for him."
2. "Absenteeism has become a problem in one of our divisions. Managers tell me that they are lax with discipline because they do not want people to quit. I know it is hard to hire people but I'm worried about ignoring our attendance policy."
3. "Volume in one of our service units has declined dramatically. We need to close the unit now, but if we do, we will have to lay off a group of good

employees." Most such decisions involve trade-offs. As one authority put it, "Management decisions do not burn cleanly. They usually produce some good results and some not-so-good effects."

I offer three guidelines for judging the effectiveness of decisions.

Did the Decision Improve Overall Performance?

A decision may produce performance increases or decreases or no change. If outcomes decline, the decision failed this test. Organizations can ill afford decisions that put performance in the tank.

Some managers argue that their decision improved an individual's performance. But if overall performance slides downhill, the big picture is still ugly. Likewise, a decision that marginally improves performance in one department but causes debilitating grief for another department fails the "improved performance" test.

Did the Decision Cause Employee Morale to Increase?

The leader's most important responsibility is to produce good performance. I understand that it is possible to achieve high performance at the expense of low employee morale in the short run. But, in the long run, if morale drops off the table, good employees flee the scene quickly.

Sometimes, the right decision may slap morale in the face in the short run while boosting overall morale in the long run. If, after a reasonable time, employee morale increases, the decision passes the second test for effectiveness.

Does the Leader Feel an Inner Peace about the Decision?

The third test for decision effectiveness is an intuitive—inner, gut-level—sense of how the leaders feel about the results. In short, is there peace of mind and a calm stomach after the decision?

While intuitive feel may not be science, I think it is a criterion of decision effectiveness. A decision, especially in a period of high stress, should produce some relief. Leaders who feel more burdened after a decision will likely struggle and flounder when executing the decision through the maze of obstacles that is sure to pop up.

When approaching complex decisions, I suggest that you apply the guidelines to the anticipated outcome. To be effective, the decision must pass all three tests. Two out of three is only 67 percent and that is failing on most measures.

C. Try to Avoid Compromises with Employees

"I like to work with my staff. If they disagree with what I think we should be doing, I'll try to meet them half way," explained a manager.

This leader has compromised. His intent may have been to get employee support, to get buy-in, and to maintain a happy atmosphere at work.

When you have disagreements with staff members, to what extent do you tend to agree with the following?

1. I might accept a little less than what I actually ask for.
2. Often, it is necessary for both of us to give a little.
3. If I can get most of what I want, I'll take it.
4. I assume that the employee will settle for a little less.

The four statements above describe a compromising approach to decision making. I define a "compromise" as an agreement where both parties gave up something to get an agreement. I understand that compromises are sometimes necessary, but good leaders try to avoid them.

Why "Compromise" is NOT a Good Strategy

The comment, "You just don't know how to compromise," commonly heard when people are locked in disagreements, is intended to be a criticism. It suggests that the other party is about as flexible as a steel pipe.

Conversely, the comment, "I have a great boss. She is willing to compromise," suggests someone who dispenses justice with the efficacy of a wise sage.

There appears to be a need for compromise when managers disagree with bosses, employees, or with each other. "Compromise" is also a strategy we use to settle conflicts with vendors, customers, union negotiators and regulators.

I suggest, however, that compromise is a poor strategy for settling most disagreements. Why? Because compromise suggests that both parties give up part of the benefit.

As in, "I want to paint it red, you want to paint it green. I don't like green, you don't like red. OK, let's compromise. How about red and green striped?" This result pleases neither of us, even though we can live with it.

I have also noted that a compromise approach suggests that you begin with an offer that you know the other will not accept. Negotiations then become a dance of wits to haggle out a payoff; and usually, at the other's expense.

All of this maneuvering consumes time and money. But the greatest cost is distrust, which results from bluff and deception that combatants employ.

Rather than Compromise, Just Try to Solve the Problem

Instead of compromise, think "problem solving"—a very different approach.

In problem solving, rivals begin by agreeing. They agree on the problem. They agree to consider alternatives. They agree to evaluate the alternatives. The intent is to find the alternative that has the greatest benefit for all parties.

Problem solvers also tacitly agree to be honest with each other and to trust each other. Above all, both parties understand that they are not big enough, bad enough, mean enough or smart enough to continuously get another person to give them more and accept less.

Compromises have become so embedded in our culture that the first response to problem-solving may be skepticism. However, employees soon learn that problem solving leaders mean what they say.

As one follower expressed, "Our new boss is more direct. When she tells you something, you can count on it. Although she has only been here three months, our bickering and whining have declined. Morale and performance have increased."

D. Avoid Participative Decision Making Mistakes

"I don't understand why my staff members are upset. I get them involved in all of our major decisions," explained a perplexed manager. "Yet, they still say that they do not have enough say-so in how I run the department."

In private discussion, subordinates stated the manager frequently squelched debate by aggressively questioning subordinate suggestions.

"Whenever I attempt to make a recommendation," explained a chagrined staff member. "he grills me like I was a suspect in a crime. After awhile, I just quit giving him ideas."

Below are other common managerial mistakes in implementing participative decision making.

Don't Make Subordinates Guess What You are Thinking

Many leaders have strong opinions on issues. It is OK to have strong opinions; but some opinionated leaders, under the name of participation, withhold their position and ask for recommendations.

When subordinates offer something that, from the leader's perspective, seems to come from left field, the leader promptly rejects the idea. In the next breath, the leader asks the staff member to come back with another recommendation.

Subordinates quickly get the idea that the leader has already figured out how to solve the problem. All he now wants is for his staff to read his mind and submit the "correct" answer. This builds distrust and frustration.

Don't Give the Illusion that All Will Agree with the Decision

"I'm not going to make a decision until we all agree on the approach we want to take," stated a consensus-oriented manager. Consensus building is desirable, but it is impractical for most solutions.

A consensus decision means that everyone in the group agrees with the approach. We respect diverse ideas and suggestions, but it is highly unlikely that a group of more than two or three people will agree completely on how to resolve any complex problem. The result of required consensus, all too often, is delay and failure to reach a conclusion. Or, dissenting members give in just to get the item off the agenda. During implementation dissenters frequently impede progress.

Don't Ask for Advice Unless You Are Willing to Take it

"I used to offer a lot of suggestions," said a staff member, "but I can't remember the last time that she took any of my advice."

When leaders ask for suggestions, it is natural to assume that the leader will take into account all or some of the advice given to her. But as a practical matter, it is impossible to take all of the advice of any group; thus, some members feel misled.

Participation implies that leaders demonstrate their sincerity by actually using some of the suggestions of others. If you ask for suggestions, it is necessary to sometimes actually take the advice and use it to help frame solutions.

To achieve effective participation in decision-making, consider the following suggestions:

1. Do ask for subordinate input into complex decisions.
2. Avoid making up your mind until you have received suggestions.
3. If you have opinions, reveal them up front.
4. Let staff members disagree without arguing or debating with them.
5. Try to find a way to accept the input of some staff members.
6. When you accept input, report clearly where the input came from.
7. Let staff members know that it is OK to disagree with you.
8. Look upon all suggestions as helpful.
9. Carefully explain any options that are off the table.
10. Let people know that you will be unable to implement all suggestions.

Under the right conditions, staff members want to give their insights to leaders. Leaders who effectively use participation typically make better decisions.

E. Participative Decision Making
May Set Up Delusional Expectations

I have asked hundreds of managers the following question, "Do you think your organization is in need of 'more direction' or 'more participation' in decision making?"

Almost three out of four respondents answer, "More participation."

I think the concept of "participative decision making" is confusing and often ineffective.

I ask managers and employees, "What does participation mean to you?"

"It means that we get together and discuss important decisions. Leaders listen to our suggestions," is a typical response.

"Does it mean you vote on the important issues?"

"No, we don't vote; we give our recommendations. We don't all agree ourselves."

How does the leader then decide? Does she go with the majority or the most vocal? Does she seek compromises? What if the leader believes that the best decision is one that most of the group recommends against? Does she have to go along with the group? Is it participative leadership when a leader goes against the majority?

Participation often Creates Unrealistic Expectations

Here is the problem. When a leader says he/she seeks participation, most subordinates leap to the conclusion that they are the decision makers. This is unrealistic.

You cannot get five subordinates—and certainly not twenty-five or thirty—to agree on a simple thing like what brand of coffee to buy for the office or what are good reasons for missing work.

For more complex decisions like what software system to buy, changes in product design, whether to drop a service, or how best to beat the competition, agreement is about as likely as pigs flying.

Here is the trap. ALL subordinates think they are going to have a major influence on the decision, yet it is impossible for all subordinates to agree. Therefore, no matter what the decision, many people will not like it.

People feel betrayed and say things like, "He didn't like my suggestion. It'll be a long time before he gets another one from me." "If he already had his mind made up, why did he waste my time?"

Subordinates who "lost" band together in the hallways and parking lots and bemoan their defeat. Certainly, they do not feel committed to the decision.

Should the decision actually prove ineffective, some losers take pride in saying, "I told you so!" or "If you had listened to me back in February, this would never have happened."

I Suggest that You Lose the Word, "Participation"

I think we should lose the word "participative decision making" and its cousin "participative leadership."

Communicate to your staff, "As the leader, it is my responsibility to make final decisions." Of course, ask subordinates for suggestions. But do not allow people to assume that they are going to make the decision.

Try this. Work up a tentative plan and present your idea as a proposal. Then ask your staff to critique your proposal. Listen with an open mind. When you get an improvement, accept it on the spot and thank the participant.

When you get recommendations that do not advance your proposal, listen patiently, explain briefly your concern, and thank the person for his suggestion. Move on. Do not belabor the issue.

Effective decisions are made by individuals, not groups. Do listen to staff input, but all should know that the leader alone is responsible for the decision.

When subordinates realize their leader makes clean and clear decisions, three good things happen. One, you get quicker decisions. Two, you actually get better support for your decisions. Three, you get better decisions.

F. Leaders Get "Buy-in" by Asking Employees to Do What They Are Capable of Doing

Which of the following has the greatest impact in getting staff commitment (buy-in) to decisions?

1. Allow people who have to execute the decision to participate in the decision.
2. Ask people to do what they are capable of doing.
3. Survey everyone's opinions about the decision.
4. Ask employees to commit to the decision or leave.
5. Strive for consensus decisions.

It is crucial for leaders to get commitment to important decisions.

"Buy-in" Means that People are Willing to Commit

"Buy-in" means that people support the decision. They think it is the right thing to do. They believe in their heart of hearts that the decision will return desired results.

When a leader gets "buy-in," her staff will follow her over the wall. Obstacles and setbacks are just minor challenges along the way to success. An occasional failure is just something to overcome.

It is easy to follow the leader's decisions when things are going well.

But true leaders know how to get commitment (buy-in) when the going gets tough.

I agree with one leader who said, "During the execution of a tough decision, there will be times when people wonder if it is all worth it. At that moment, the team's commitment is what counts."

I have seen committed groups perform successfully even when the decision might not have been the best. And I've seen correct decisions abandoned prior to achieving desired results. Several members of the staff just quit on the decision.

Participation Does Not Ensure Buy-in

Staff participation in decisions may be appropriate. It may even be helpful. But participation in and of itself does not insure buy-in. In fact, participation sometimes results in a fracas among team members because they hold opposing opinions.

Further, in the name of participation, leaders may simply accept what their followers offer. I have heard leaders explain their acceptance of bad suggestions by saying, "I thought it was important to get buy-in."

Another risk of participation is that some followers give poor suggestions. When the leader does not follow the suggestion, the member may pout while exclaiming, "I gave you suggestions like you asked, but you did not listen to me."

Two Ways Real Leaders Get Followers to Buy-in

In my opinion, effective leaders gain their followers' buy-in in two major ways.

One, ask followers to do what they can do. Leaders get buy-in by asking people to do what the leader knows they are capable of doing. Gordon Bethune, former CEO of Continental Airlines, says, "You've got to call the plays that the team is capable of running."

If you ask people to do things they are not capable of performing, you simply ensure failure. I do not know how they know it, but I know that leaders are aware of what their people are capable of accomplishing. Confident leaders have the courage to ask them to do it.

Two, ask people who do not join up to leave. It may seem harsh to ask people who are not willing to commit to the decision to leave the organization.

But it is unfair to allow one or two staff members to jeopardize the success of the total group simply by not committing to the leader's decision.

I do not believe that subordinates can be successful by fighting their leader's decision. If the leader asks me to do something that I am capable of doing (assuming that the request is legal, ethical and moral), I should do it. If the leader asks me to do something that I am not capable of doing, I will probably be better off in another organization.

G. How to Get Your Team to Support Tough Decisions

When you leave a meeting, how confident are you that all members of your team will support your decisions?

Some decisions are tough. Some are controversial. Still, to be an effective team, all members must line up to support decisions made by the team leader.

Does this mean that members should support the decision, even if they personally oppose it?

Unless the decision is unethical, illegal or immoral, the answer is a resounding, "Yes!"

Effective leaders use a number of measures to ensure total team support.

Ask Team Members to do Only What They are Capable of Doing

First, team members must be capable of executing the decision. They must have the skills, ability, and knowledge to perform the functions necessary to accomplish the result.

If a coach were to ask all members of a team to jump ten feet high, there would be little support for this decision. Further the team would fail. They simply do not have the ability to accomplish the feat.

Similarly, a vice president who asks for a 50 percent improvement in productivity with no changes in strategies or resources should not expect team support.

Make Clear Decisions

All team members must be able to clearly understand the decision.

Avoid terms like, "significant improvement," "watch our costs more closely," "make some gains in the market," and "may have to eventually seek some cut-backs."

Use precise terms, for example, "Five percent growth for the year," "new software operational by October 10," "compliance with new reporting policy by the beginning of the third quarter."

Vague decisions with a lot of "ifs," "ands" and "wherefores" are hard to support. They may even be hard to understand.

Encourage Passionate Debate

In the process of making tough decisions, encourage passionate debate from all team members. Intense and persuasive encounters are good things.

As the leader, be sure you listen to the debate. When others bring good points to the floor, adopt them as part of the decision. But do not modify the decision simply to appease someone.

Above all, avoid trying to reach a consensus among all members of your team. Attempts at consensus lead to weakened and compromised solutions.

As one wit said, "People need to have their say. They know that they will not always get their way."

Most team members can support a position they oppose if they had a good chance to present their case.

Communicate Beyond the Team

Discuss what should be reported outside the team.

Then, ask all team members to personally communicate to their staff members and associates.

Since the expectation is public knowledge, everyone is more likely to be operating off the same page.

Continuous Status Reporting

During execution of the decision, the leader should require all team members to give regular status updates of how the implementation is proceeding in their areas.

You can do this at the beginning of your regular meetings.

Note, this is not a time for negotiation. It is not appropriate for team members to come to a meeting with a notebook filled with excuses on why something is not happening.

Team members are to give brief status updates. If one person is behind, he or she is expected to offer suggestions for catching up.

Other team members can also offer different alternatives for getting back on the schedule. When appropriate, other members can express disappointment.

Chapter 9: Motivate

◆

(If you want a highly motivated work group, hire motivated people.)

More than 85 percent of managers who attend my workshops say that they have at least one employee who is poorly motivated.

There are more theories and more research on employee motivation than any other leadership topic. Still, most managers become flummoxed in their efforts to "jack up" some of their employees.

Most experts say that employees have needs for such things as security, companionship, growth, pride, and self-fulfillment. Thus, people work to satisfy their needs. Motivation becomes a simple matter of appealing to employee needs.

But motivation is not that simple. Some employees strive to achieve no matter how badly they are led. Others make only the slightest of commitments when working for outstanding leaders.

Here is the summarized, cliff notes version of motivation. If you want motivated employees, hire people who are already internally motivated. You cannot be an effective leader if you operate under the ill-conceived assumption that, if you persist long enough, you can find a way to motivate anyone.

Since few of us have the opportunity of selecting only highly-motivated persons, we have to do the best we can with the team that we have. Our intuition says we can get improvements by motivating marginal employees to do better. Actual practice yells at us to spend more time motivating employees who are already highly motivated.

A. Create an Environment that Encourages Motivated Employees to Flourish

Do you have any employees who...

...do not work as hard as you would like?

...take longer than they should to complete a job?

...make more mistakes than you would like?

...fail to take an initiative when problems occur?

...are quick with excuses when deadlines are not met?

If you responded "yes" to even one of these items, chances are you would like suggestions for how to better motivate employees.

Accept the Reality that You Cannot Motivate Lazy People

Most of us would like to get inside the heads of a couple of our staff members and tighten the loose screws. But in reality, no matter how good our leadership skills, you cannot turn rocks into gold and you cannot, as a practical matter, motivate adults against their wishes. Hear this, "Leaders do not motivate people."

If you wish to put your motivational prowess to the test, hire a couple of lazy, stubborn, hardheaded, self-serving employees and try to turn them into dynamic, cooperative team players. I will bet the farm that you will fail.

It is possible to motivate most anyone, if you have the wherewithal to inflict severe punishment. You could also motivate people if you had the pot of gold at the end of the rainbow and you were willing to pay huge sums of dollars for people to do things.

If you want a motivated work group, do what the brightest managers have been doing for years. Hire people who are already highly motivated!

Managers Can Create an Environment Where Motivated People Can Thrive

While leaders cannot motivate others, they can create an environment where self-motivated people can thrive.

Here is what is needed in a motivational environment:

• Everyone should know clearly what is expected.

- People should have the necessary materials and equipment to do their jobs.
- Strong doses of positive reinforcement should be given when people make a contribution.
- An opportunity to share in the financial gains of the organization should be made available.

Add these four stimulating ingredients to an internally driven staff and you will have a highly motivated work group.

What to Do for Those Who Do Not Respond to the Environment

Granted, it is nigh impossible to hire a complete staff that is highly charged. Further, many leaders do not have the opportunity to pick and choose exactly who they want.

So, most leaders have an employee problem or two. It is important to deal with problems appropriately. Consider the following guidelines.

1. Check to see if the employee needs training. If so, provide it.
2. Determine whether you can effectively assign the problem part of the work to someone else.
3. If neither training nor reassignments are practical or helpful, determine whether the employee problem is a nuisance or a major distraction.
4. If the problem is a nuisance, get over it and quit worrying about it. The world is not perfect.
5. If the problem is a major distraction, do what you must, legally and ethically, to separate the individual from the organization.

While good leaders do not technically motivate people, they do make intensive efforts to create an environment that invites motivated people to do their best.

B. Motivate Good Employees by Ensuring that Most of Your Feedback is Seen as Positive

"Thank you." "Keep it up." "Good job." "You're getting better." "That's true." "Excellent idea." "Fine." "I like it." "I appreciate it." "I'm pleased." "It's an improvement." "I'm proud of you." "Quick learner." "You've got it."

How frequently do you use these, or similar, examples of verbal positive reinforcement? Most employees say, "Not nearly enough!"

What about the more subtle, nonverbal reinforces—smiling, grinning, thumbs up, firm handshake, eye contact, nodding agreement, laughing, clapping hands, listening? Not enough of these either.

Unfortunately, Most Management Feedback is Negative

Employees in my surveys say that 80 percent of the feedback they receive from their managers is negative.

Why is this? Partly because managers tend to focus on what needs fixing rather than what is right. Secondly, many managers are not aware that some of their feedback is seen as negative.

Take an example of coaching. A manager said to a new employee, "Here, let me show you. If you will do it this way you will be more accurate."

The manager is being helpful, offering good suggestions. Positive, right? Well, not really. Most employees consider this to be negative. Why? The manager obviously did not approve of what the employee was doing.

Take another example: performance reviews. Reviewers spend most time on what needs to be improved. Little time is spent on highly rated factors.

Further, common language—rejects, behind schedule, rework, customer complaints, absentee rate, down time, missed deadlines, error rates, scrape rate, turnover rate—also contributes to the negative mist in too many work places.

The Most Powerful Motivator is Sincere Praise

Verbal and nonverbal positive reinforcement is both the most powerful and most underused external motivator.

Author Claude Steiner says that most people live with "stroke deficit." That is, they do not receive nearly enough positive strokes. Author and consultant, Ken Blanchard, writes that managers need to spend more time, "...catching their employees doing something right." Countless surveys suggest that employees are literally starved for appreciation and praise. In the absence of frequent positive feedback, a negative fog envelopes employees.

Most employees do most things right most of the time. If not, you could not stay in business. I believe that most managers understand the importance of showing appreciation. They are just so intent on getting to perfection that mistakes become their focus.

When I ask managers if too much praise might be ineffective, about 60 percent respond, "Yes." When I ask how many have received too much praise within the last year, no one raises a hand. Of course, one dose of phony and insincere praise intended to manipulate is too much. But we are a long way from giving too much sincere praise for good work.

Some people believe that they should only praise extraordinary accomplishments. As they say, "We do not want to cheapen our appreciation." But look at how we behave at sporting events. We clap and cheer and roar dozens of times during a single event. I am aware of no case where a team began to perform poorly because their supporters cheered too loudly or too often.

I say even if the improvement is only slight, reinforce it. If you catch marginal employees leaning in the right direction, give them a pat on the back.

Do I suggest that you ignore mistakes, absenteeism, rework, and missed targets? No, no and no! The suggestion is simply this: "You can be more effective by finding more ways to praise more people more often."

C. Motivate High Performers by Spending More Time with Them

"Do you spend more of your time with marginal or high performing employees?" is a question that I frequently ask managers. About 73 percent of respondents say they spend more time with their marginal performers. I ask, "Why?"

Typical responses include, "They need more help." "I take pride in developing people." "The best way to improve your group is to improve your weaker performers." "A chain is only as strong as its weakest link."

Most people like to help others whom they believe to be less capable. We root for slower, less talented athletic teams. Long shots. Dark horses. We rejoice mightily when underdogs win.

Chances Are, You Give Ample Support to Marginal Producers

I agree that it is proper and admirable to train, coach and mentor below average workers. Likewise, problem employees who rail against policies need and deserve help.

I also think most below average producers and policy violators get a lot of support.

I ask managers, "What do you do about employees who make too many mistakes or take too long to complete their jobs?" Most managers say they stress employee develop programs, patient coaching and training.

What about employees who miss a lot of work? Distract others? Ignore policies? Disagree excessively with decisions? Complain endlessly?

"We try to find out what their problem is and help them. We give a lot of chances before we fire people," said a manager.

"We have an Employee Assistance Program," explained another manager. "Employees can get professional help with drinking and drug addictions, marital relationships, financial woes, emotional depression, job burnout—you name it."

I Suggest It Is Your Top Performers Who Would Benefit from More of Your Support

I do not suggest reducing support for marginal employees. I do suggest dramatically increasing support for high performers, for two reasons.

One, you will get better results. Two, while they may not actually need your support, they have certainly earned it.

You are far more likely to get ten percent improvement from top performers than you are from marginal workers. As one wit said, "If you get ten-percent improvement from a marginal employee, you still ain't got nothing."

Traditionally, we support top performers with better performance reviews, higher earnings, and more consideration for promotions. All of this is good. Add the following to the mix.

1. Bestow special titles and status on high producing stars. It may not be necessary to promote them to management. Many high performers would rather do what they are doing than assume a managerial role.
2. Select good performers who are good teachers and create special roles so that they can teach and train others.
3. Make available high status training programs for only those performers who perform at a certain level.

4. Informally organize high performers to become advisors to you. Seek their input when making significant decisions.

5. Consider allowing a group of high performers to serve as "change agents." Give them special assignments when introducing new things.

Staff members who commit themselves to the mission, perform well, and avoid petty, distracting office politics are extremely valuable. Peers respect such key performers. They are often informal leaders. I, for one, am inclined to show them a healthy dose of professional favoritism.

D. Overcome Your Reservations and Recognize Top Performers

Some managers show about as much enthusiasm for recognizing top performers as they do for a county fair turtle race.

"I complimented an employee recently," explained a manager. "His response was, 'Do I get a pay raise?'"

"How did you respond?" I asked.

"I was so befuddled, I just stuttered something about how it seemed like all people cared about anymore was their pay raise."

Sadly, less than 30 percent of top performers feel fully appreciated. I understand that some employees may not feel appreciated even if their managers staged a parade in their honor. I am also aware that too many managers are reluctant to show public recognition to their most outstanding performers.

Why Should I Pat Them on the Back When They Are Getting Paid?

"Why should I have to pat them on the back all of the time?" asked a manager.

"That's what they're getting paid to do."

Employees do get paid. But a pat on the back costs nothing. If we are willing to pay money to do a job, it makes no sense to me that we would withhold recognition and privileges.

If I Praise Too Much, Employees Will "Let Down"

"I never let my employees think that I'm satisfied with what they do. If I compliment them too much, they'll slack off on you."

This sentiment is contradictory to all that we know about human behavior. Recall a time when a teacher or coach publicly recognized you for a good grade or an outstanding play to win the game. Did the recognition make you want to rest on your laurels? Certainly not. What it did was to energize you to work harder.

I'm Not Sure Who My Top Performers Are

One manager explained, "It's hard to know who my top performers are because all of my people do different jobs."

If you do not know who your top performers are, I say you are not an observant manager. You may not have objective performance measures that you can easily compare. Still, you can recognize top performers. They are the ones with great attitudes who do outstanding work. So what if it is just your subjective judgment? As the leader, your judgment counts. Everyone else in the group also knows who they are as well.

Here is a good test. If you had to lay off all employees but one, who would you keep? That person has got to be one of your best performers.

What if the Person I Recognize is Not a Good Performer Next Month?

"I can't grant the window office to my best performer. That person may not be the best performer next quarter. Do I rotate offices every quarter?"

Where do people get such beliefs? Performance is very stable and very predictable. The odds are exceptionally high that a good performer today was a good performer five years ago. And she will be a good performer five years from now.

If I Pay too much Attention to My Performers, others Complain

This one frustrates me the most. "If I pay too much attention to a top performer, others will get jealous. We are a team. I can't put one person above the others."

Tell that to highly effective sports teams that have no trouble identifying "most valuable players." If you withhold recognition because you do not want others to whine, you are actually rewarding the whiners. Guess what. You get more whining.

Top performers may not actually need your recognition. They will perform whether you appreciate them or not. Then why should we make over them so much? Because they deserve it!

E. Avoid Five Typical Pitfalls When Appreciating Employees

I believe three things about employee appreciation.

One, personal appreciation from the leader is one of the more potent employee motivators.

Two, eight of ten employees believe their leaders do not fully appreciate them.

Three, even ardent boosters frequently botch their efforts to applaud employees.

Employees want to be appreciated. Leaders know that appreciation is effective. Yet, leaders frequently stumble in their efforts to show gratitude. Below are five common pitfalls.

1. Ignoring small achievements. "Why should I make a big deal about employees coming to work and doing their job?" questioned a manager. "That's what I pay them to do."

True, we do pay employees to show up and do their work. In fact, some are paid pretty well. So my response is, "If you are willing to pay employees good money to do a job, why aren't you also willing to give them an occasional pat-on-the-back as well."

After all, appreciation costs no money and a simple "thank you" is easy to deliver. Further, sincere appreciation, even for small improvements, causes good employees to work even harder. And it encourages some poor performers to seek the boss's attention by doing their jobs better.

2. Not linked to performance. "Why did you bring bagels to the office today?" I asked. "Because it's Friday," came the response.

A bagel on Friday is not a bad thing. It is just not linked to performance. It is far more effective to bring bagels because the team has successfully completed a major project, or because performance was outstanding.

3. Not being sensitive to how employees like to receive appreciation. After a service team had an outstanding quarter, the manager said, "To show my appreciation, I'm buying a pancake and sausage breakfast for the whole team on Friday morning."

Later Friday morning, the manager asked an employee, "How do you think everyone enjoyed the breakfast?"

"Ah, we don't usually eat breakfast," replied the employee. "We had to get up an hour early."

"Well if we do this again next quarter, what would you like?" asked the manager.

"Beer and pizza," said the employee.

Next quarter, the manager bought beer and pizza for the top team. The event was a big hit. The lesson is: To be effective, leaders must show appreciation in the way that employees want to receive it.

4. Appreciation efforts become too routine. When managers have success with appreciation efforts, they naturally wish to repeat them. That is how company programs such as employee-of-the-month evolved.

However, successful one-time efforts often lose their value when we turn them into routine, structured company programs. Institutionalized programs, to many, do not seem sincere and they are not personal. Some even get mired down in office politics.

5. Appreciation with little enthusiasm. Some leaders seem fearful of praising with enthusiasm. "You know, if we make too much of a fuss, others will get jealous and complain," confided a manager.

I say, "So what." I do not think we want to let low-performing, jealous, and critical employees have that much influence on our practices.

Appreciation efforts do not seem sincere unless leaders are genuinely excited about showing their thankfulness. Recipients need to hear the enthusiasm in their leaders' voices and see it in their faces. If a marginal employee gets upset, so be it.

It is hard work to sincerely communicate appreciation to employees, but successful efforts pay huge dividends. In addition, it is the right thing to do.

F. Motivate Problem Employees by Appealing to Pride and Self Respect

"How do you handle employees who are performing below standards?" I asked a manager.

The manager responded, "I discuss the problem and make suggestions for improvement."

"What do you do if you get no improvement?"

"If the problem is bad enough, I'll put the employee on a plan with specific things to accomplish."

When I ask problem employees how their manager tries to motivate them, I get comments like: "He just comes over and complains about something I haven't done." "My manager is never satisfied. It doesn't matter what I do." "They don't try to motivate us. They just gripe about taking too long to do a job or say we make too many mistakes."

When dealing with employees who are stale, embittered, slow, or make more mistakes than an inexperienced rookie, I agree that managers should explain their dissatisfaction and ask them to do better.

But I think something is missing and that is an appeal to the employee's pride. Most employees, even problematic ones, have some pride. If you can tap into the pride, you just may get the employee's commitment to do better.

How to Appeal to Pride and Self Respect

Pride is self respect, a feeling of personal worth, as in "I take pride in who I am and what I do." When correcting an employee, after pointing out your dissatisfaction, appeal to the employee's pride. Consider the following…

Highlight Credentials.

Review the employee's work experience, degrees and training. For instance, "You have 18 years of experience in the industry and you have your certification. Sixty percent of the industry does not. You seldom miss work."

Note Positive Character Attributes.

Identify positive character traits, such as, "I know that you will always say what is on your mind." Or, "When you say you will do something, I can take that to the bank." Or, "Other employees follow your lead because they have respect for your opinions."

Review Accomplishments.

For performances that may have hit the wall, look for historical accomplishments. Find something that the employee has done well. Has the employee completed any part of the work satisfactorily? Is there an example of a good response from other customers or other departments? Has she ever had a good suggestion?

Pick out something that the employee has done and work that into your coaching effort.

Show Confidence in the Employee's Abilities.

Let the employee know that you think he has the ability to do what you are asking him to do, such as, "I know you have the ability to deliver what this customer wants. The customer is very important. We are all counting on you."

Be Aware of Nonverbal Messages

You must get voice tone and body language right if you want employees to hear the nobler reaches of your message.

Note how voice tone changes the meaning in the following, simple sentence. "*I* did not steal the watch." (I understand it was stolen. I did not do it.) "I did not *steal* the watch." (I found it, borrowed it, bought it, but did not steal it.) "I did not steal the *watch*." (I got the camera, the money, the jewelry, but not the watch.)

When appealing to pride, use a pleasant tone. Emphasize positive words. Allow voice inflection when expressing confidence. Maintain a pleasant facial expression and good body posture.

Employees' hearing improves significantly when you personalize your message by appealing to pride and delivering it in a pleasant tone with confident expressions.

G. Motivate Employees by Treating Each Person Differently

When it comes to employees, an accepted guideline is, "Treat everyone the same."

But I think the really astute leaders follow a different principle and treat employees as individuals.

Some employees like public praise. Public praise embarrasses some employees. Some employees desire more autonomy. Other employees prefer close supervision. Some employees like risky assignments. Risky assignments scare some employees. Some people like to work in groups. Other people like more independent work.

"Treat Everyone the Same," is Not Fair Treatment

Most managers desire to treat employees fairly. Yet, "favoritism" and "unfairness" are two common employee complaints. Why do both of these conditions exist? It is not because managers lack the wisdom of Solomon. Rather many managers, I believe, confuse "sameness" with "fairness."

For instance, a manager recently reported, "I don't know why my employees think I play favorites, I treat everyone exactly alike."

However, all employees are not exactly alike; aptitudes, motivation, and personalities differ dramatically. Likewise, contribution to departmental goals and teamwork also differ. In the eyes of employees, to treat everyone exactly alike is to treat many people unfairly.

Each Employee Has a Unique Personality

Consider the personality dimension. Some personalities may be "soft." That is, harsh voice tones, sharp criticism and rough kidding hurt deeply. Soft personalities respond well to mild suggestions and subtle coaching.

Under supportive conditions, "soft personalities" develop and grow. Give them time and they may learn to produce.

Other personalities are "hard" or "thick-skinned." "Hard personalities" can rebound from sharp attacks and vigorous goading more easily.

It may be appropriate for managers to "rattle some cages" to get the attention of "hard personalities." Without control, these employees may learn to claim resources for their own purposes with little regard of what is best for the department. Other employees, between the two extremes, develop best with a touch of support balanced with skillful direction and control.

Some Employees May Perceive Different Treatment as "Unfair"

When you treat people differently according to their uniqueness, someone may comment, "You didn't give me the same chance you gave Mary Ann!"

A good response might be, "I do not treat everyone the same, but I am fair."

Treat Employees Differently because It Is the Fair Thing to Do

Two guidelines for people treatment appear to serve leaders well.

One, because we are all unique individuals, no one rule can apply effectively to all. Rather than treating everyone the same, effective leaders seem to instinctively know who and when to "stroke" as well as when to "apply the spurs."

Two, I believe that individuals earn different treatment. Effective leaders may be very professional when dealing with both high and low performers, but they do treat high performers differently than low performers.

High performers earn more responsibility, respect and money. Lower performers deserve respect as human beings, but they may not deserve the same considerations as higher performers.

Consider the following do's and do not's:

Do be sensitive to differences in employee personalities.

Do realize that some employees need a lot of support.

Do be aware that some employees require more direction.

Do tailor your leadership style to employee maturity levels.

Do give higher performers the benefit of the doubt.

Do not treat all employees exactly alike.

Do not try to please everyone all of the time.

Do not overreact to complaints of unfairness.

Do not over control high performers.

Do not give lesser performers as much latitude.

Remember, the goal is to treat people fairly. While the word "fair" may be subjective, in the mind of an effective leader, the concept of "fair" becomes very clear.

H. How to Effectively Use "Fear" in Motivation

King Shaka, leader of the Zulus in the 1800s, imposed fearful discipline on his followers. When people made mistakes, he had them shot. To impress a visiting chieftain, Shaka once ordered a squad to march off a cliff to their deaths. Not a single soldier hesitated.

Many writers proclaim that employees work best in secure environments. Employees, the thesis goes, are more creative, more relaxed and they perform better when they feel confident in their positions.

Yet, we see examples in crisis situations where fear caused adrenaline to pump such that people perform extraordinary physical feats. Some entrepreneurs report that they persisted through tough times because they were afraid of failure.

I believe that immense fear freezes some people into inaction or panicked decisions that turn out badly. I think some people get anxiety attacks more easily than others.

For some people, fear of making a mistake may actually create more errors. (Recall, how your performance worsened when your typing teacher watched over your shoulder as you were learning typing skills.)

Yet, I think effective leaders understand that proper use of fear can be a constructive performance tool.

Employees Should Fear the Consequences of Poor Performance

Many leaders who do not perform to expectations fear loss of their jobs. And, in many cases, the fear is appropriate.

In justification, a CEO said, "It's simple. If managers don't perform, I do not have a company. I give them all the training and support the company can afford, but I'm up front with them about what they need to accomplish if we are to survive."

Failure of the company to perform, as in financial losses, can strike fear in leaders and employees at all levels.

I encourage leaders to use all of the positive financial and nonfinancial incentives for inducing high performance. Appropriate hiring is crucial. Training is a great aid. Positive reinforcement is effective. Many make bonuses work.

Still, at some point, effective leaders and employees become aware that they have to outperform their competitors or they lose their benefits and their jobs.

Employees Should Fear the Consequences of Not Making Necessary Changes

We've gone from 80K personal computers to "Windows" in less than 20 years. In most organizations, it is the failure to change that generates the fear.

"As a company, we either change and adapt or die," is the way one leader put it.

Successful organizations constantly evolve their products and services. Mergers and acquisitions appear always on the horizon. Structural relationships and policies change more rapidly than hair styles.

Today's leaders must execute changes efficiently and quickly. Managers constantly seek remedies for overcoming resistance to change, and they arm themselves with the latest and greatest theories of how to be a change agent.

The means to overcome resistance sometimes is "fear," as in, "Do you want to make this change, or do you want me to put someone else in your position who will make the change?"

Employees Should Fear the Consequences of Disagreeing Too Much

Different ideas, disagreements, and multiple alternatives are good to a point. Debates about how to improve can lead to enlightened decisions. Effective problem solving encourages the consideration of views different from my own.

But, as a sensible leader said, "After we've had our disagreements, we have to quit arguing about who has the best idea and unify our efforts around a common solution."

Successful coaches actually kick people off their teams if they argue and disagree too much. Managers do too. An environment where too much disagreement creates fear of being removed may be a good thing.

I agree that too much fear in a group is probably unworkable, but the total absence of fear is also not effective.

Chapter 10: Teamwork

✦

(Talented individuals are even more effective when they work as a team.)

What a beautiful thing it is to watch teamwork among players on a highly ranked basketball team. When a team has good chemistry, it can often beat a group of individuals who may run faster and jump higher. Teamwork is just as important in business as it is in sports, says Lee Iacocca, the CEO who led Chrysler Corporation out of bankruptcy a few decades ago.

People in organizations belong to several teams. Employees of the same department are members of the departmental team. Some employees also serve on task forces, committees, or project teams. The frontline supervisor is the leader of a team. She is also the member of a team of peer supervisors which is led by their manager.

All organizations, large and small, require people working together to achieve a common goal and that spells "teamwork." As one wit commented, "There is no 'I' in teamwork."

A. Voluntary Cooperation is Teamwork; Finger Pointing is Not

Teamwork is a wonderful thing. When people function as a unit, they can often accomplish more than highly talented individuals who are not working as a team. I would, without question, prefer working with a highly motivated team player over a more talented self-serving individual.

The results of efficient teamwork are magical. People working as teams produce better quality, lower costs, happier customers and higher profits. Unfortunately, not all managers understand team behaviors. Some managers, under the guise of encouraging teamwork, actually suppress group solidarity and performance.

For instance, a manager says, "Jane is not a team player."

Jane's response was, "My manager thinks that 'team play' means that we support every off-centered idea that he comes up with."

Most of us are team players in our own minds. Yet, some managers misinterpret what team play is.

Team Players Put the Good of the Team Ahead of their Personal Ambitions

Team play is a willingness to make individual sacrifices and to inconvenience one's self for the good of the total group. Some aspects of team play are easy to understand, for instance:

- Helping others with their work
- Covering for each other on breaks
- Volunteering to share boring jobs
- Supporting less experienced people on tough jobs
- Staying over to help another shift
- Coaching slower performers
- Trading days off
- Staying over to finish a project
- Supporting the boss when you agree

Other aspects of team play are less obvious, such as:

- Requesting only the budget you need
- Volunteering to return part of your budget when other departments need support
- Taking salary or benefit cuts when the organization sustains losses
- Supporting a peer who got a promotion you aspired to
- Disagreeing with the boss when you honestly believe the decision to be hurtful to the organization
- Executing changes you do not totally support

Anti Team Players put their Individual Aspirations ahead of the Group

An attitude of "What's in it for me?" is not team play. A desire to put my department ahead of the mission of the organization is a step up from "looking out for my best interest." But it is still not team play.

Team players do not:

- Strive for undeserved credit
- Blame others for problems
- Withhold sensitive information
- Avoid accountability
- Start or perpetuate rumors
- Go along to get along
- Overly defend your failures
- Document just to cover yourself
- Allow a plan to fail just so you can be "right"
- Demand additional staff to build your empire
- Place your personal advantage above that of the organization

Good Team Players Build Good Chemistry within a Team

When a group is really "clicking," we say that the team has good chemistry. Contrarily, a team that does not work well together, we say, has bad chemistry.

What is team chemistry? It is an intangible dimension that shows up in commitment to the mission, acceptance of individual responsibilities and support for team members.

The best indicator of "team chemistry" is the behavior of a group when there is a problem. Teams with poor chemistry tend to blame each other, choose sides, and compete among themselves.

On teams with good chemistry, individuals rush to support their "fallen" members. Cooperation, support and assistance are abundant. Typically, the team member feels supported and quickly recovers—eager to help others.

B. As in Sports, Project Teams Work better when all Members Understand Their Roles

The first meeting of the new project team began politely enough. Members ambled in, greeted acquaintances, introduced themselves, and engaged in friendly chit chat.

About fifteen minutes past the starting time, the project leader announced, "This team has been formed to reduce the time that it takes for originating and placing materials' orders with new vendors."

For the next few minutes, discussions rambled to and fro without addressing any serious issues. After a bit, the project leader injected, "At our next meeting, we'll need to finalize a mission statement and we'll work on a scope of work."

After the fifth meeting, one member said to a team member in the hallway, "We meet and discuss a lot, but we can't seem to agree on anything." The member responded, "It sure takes us a long time to get anything done." The two persons also criticized other members for being unprepared, making foolish statements, and playing politics.

Members behaved politely, perhaps artificially so, during the meetings. But away from the team, members talked about each other like quarreling cousins. Unfortunately, this experience is pretty typical.

Increase Teamwork by Clearly Identifying each Member's Role

The team did the right thing by working on a mission statement and a scope of work. However, before the team began serious problem-solving efforts, I think the leader, with input from the members, should have established roles for each member.

Just as a basketball team benefits by having a designated player as point guard, another as a shooting guard, a rebounding center, and so on, project teams also benefit by identifying roles for each of its members.

One team that I am familiar with chose the following roles for its six members: team leader, technical expert, policy expert, task role, relationship role, and summarizer.

The role of the team leader was fairly traditional—organize and communicate the agenda, ensure proper meeting facilities, run the meeting, and coordinate communication between meetings.

The technical expert was the "go to" authority on technical specifications of the materials. The policy person ensured that the team had all of the information it needed on company purchasing and vendor policies.

The task role was to keep the team on schedule. This person made statements like, "We are getting off the topic." "I think we have spent enough time on this item." "We need to make a decision before three o'clock." "I think everyone needs to be better prepared for the next meeting."

The person selected for the relationship role was a popular individual. His role was to be supportive. He reduced tensions, soothed hurt feelings and mediated intense discussions.

The summarizer frequently reviewed the status of the project. She summarized the points on each side of an argument, identified areas of agreement and noted what was still left undecided. Toward the end of the meeting, she summarized the meeting and reviewed action items.

The deliberate effort to identify roles early in the project and to select specific people for each role enhances teamwork. For instance, when the task person butts into a prolonged speech and admonishes a team member to "stay on the topic," the member does not get in a snit. He knows the task person is just performing his role.

C. Teamwork Requires the Right People, a Leader and Team Training

"I'd like to schedule a two-hour session on teambuilding," stated a client.

"What do you hope to accomplish?"

"I'm trying to get my people to work together better .... to improve their teamwork."

A two-hour session on teambuilding might be fun. It might be even be enlightening. It is unlikely to create lasting improvement in teamwork.

Many people approach teamwork like it is some type of engine with a missing part. Just put the right concept in the right place, add high-grade fuel, and the group will begin to hum like a finely tuned engine. Too many leaders approach teamwork with an innocent naiveté. Some think they only need begin referring to their departments as "teams" and teamwork will magically emerge.

Teamwork occurs when individuals subordinate their personal needs and coordinate their abilities to achieve a common goal. Good team members fit their individual talents together seamlessly as they pursue a result.

A team member described her experience with a successful team, "My experience was exhilarating. We worked hard. I enjoyed it immensely. It was enjoyable .... fulfilling. We over achieved!"

Filling in, helping out, mutual respect, absolute trust and shared victories are compelling and rewarding forces. In reality, teamwork is very complex. It is very hard to create and sustain.

Teamwork Requires People Who Want to Cooperate

The first step in building teamwork is getting the right people on the team. The right people are inclined to be cooperative, helpful, trusting, and respectful.

Some individuals' personalities repel team effort like dictators ward off freedom. Very independent, self-focused, controlling, and "me first" individuals do not good teammates make.

Put differently, do not hire selfish, manipulative, deceitful, arrogant, egotistical, glory seekers with bad attitudes and expect to turn them into dynamic, supportive, accommodating, team members willing to make personal sacrifices for the good of the group. If you try this, you will fail.

Teamwork Requires Insightful Leadership

Contrary to what many people believe, it takes strong (not participative) leadership to forge effective teams. Much of the hard work of teams occurs outside of the spotlight—being available when needed, positively doing favors, doing the "grunt work" without complaint, putting egos aside and rejoicing in the success of others.

As one leader said, "Many of the efforts of good team members do not always show up in the box score. It is my responsibility to identify intangible contributions and make sure they are appreciated."

Even good team players are sometimes tempted to violate team spirit. They may put their needs first, take too much credit for successes, begrudge the success of others, or perhaps flout core values of the team's culture.

Leaders must be strong enough to rein in members who violate team values no matter how talented or capable the team member may be.

Teamwork Training Enhances Teamwork

With the right team members and the right leadership, teambuilding efforts will pay off.

Training in joint problem solving, pursuit of common goals, interpersonal communication, organization and trust building produce great results when delivered to willing participants.

The most effective training occurs continuously. Leaders serve as good examples. They take every opportunity to coach members individually. Regular meetings become, in part, training sessions. Each personal interaction becomes a learning experience.

Training can also include the more traditional reading of good books, observing training videos, or participating in development workshops.

With the right people, the right leader, the right training and a little luck, perhaps the group can personally experience the fabled slogan of the three musketeers: "One for all and all for one!"

D. Bill Russell (The Basketball Player) Explains His Rules of Teamwork

Identify the extent to which you agree or disagree with the following statements.

Successful teamwork is more likely to flourish when leaders ...

1. Listen more than talk.
2. Try to draw others out.
3. Use a benevolent dictator style.
4. Also know how to follow.
5. Make clear choices and take responsibility.
6. Make decisions quickly.

According to Bill Russell in his book, *Russell Rules: Eleven Lessons of Leadership from the Twentieth Century's Greatest Winner,* the correct response to all of these statements is "agree."

Bill Russell, who lectures frequently to corporate and governmental leaders, was a great professional basketball player and coach for the Boston Celtics. Sports writers recognize Russell as one of the greatest team players of all time in any sport.

Team Leaders Listen more than They Talk

As Russell says, "It is better to understand than to be understood."

Of course, all leaders want to be understood. Most have passion for what they do. Patience and tolerance quickly changes into stress and anxiety for individuals when others do not understand them.

It is a challenge to get diverse people to work as a team toward a common goal. It is important to listen to and understand the motives, values, suggestions, concerns, hopes and fears of each team member.

Team Leaders Draw Out the Quieter Members

Some team members are as loud as the Fourth of July. Some are as quiet as the evening sunset. All are important.

Leaders do not have to guess what verbal members are thinking. "If it comes into my head, I'm likely to say it," explained a verbal person.

Quiet people are just as thoughtful and have just as many insights. Effective leaders understand this and find ways to draw out their more shy members.

Teams Function Better Under Benevolent Dictators

Trainloads of books and boatloads of articles explain the fruits of participative leadership. In many circles, facilitation has come to mean almost the same thing as leadership.

Russell, and many serious researchers, suggest that participation is fine up to a point. But teamwork requires that leaders strive to do what is right rather than produce mediated decisions.

Benevolent dictators listen. They seriously consider suggestions from their team members. Benevolent dictators do not hold elections. They do not hold endless meetings. They do not believe that they have to go with the majority. And they do not delay a decision to get still more input.

To Lead a Team, You Must Know How to Follow

No leader, no matter how powerful or esteemed, is God. All leaders work within the context of a larger whole. Presidents of corporations report to boards of directors. Board members ultimately answer to stockholders. All serve customers.

Russell suggests that it is hard to be a good team leader without knowing how to be a good follower. Leaders who can effectively model team behaviors have more credibility.

Team Leaders Select Clear Visions and Goals

If a large number of humans (all diverse and different) are to work as a team, the group's goals and strategies must be clear.

You do not have to be the author of a thesaurus to understand a team-building leader's word choices regarding vision and goals. Teamwork requires use of the KISS principle—keep it short and simple. We might also add, "Make it clear."

Team Leaders Make Timely Decisions

The longer leaders delay important decisions, the greater the probability of staff squabbling. Delays raise doubts, make people skeptical, and allow time for members' ideas and minds to stray. Teamwork requires timely decisions.

"We can't wait at the corner for three days while the leader decides which fork in the road to take," explained an energized staff member. "After a short while, some of us are going to start out on our own."

Leaders with good teamwork, both in sports and in business, often out-perform more talented opponents who do not work well together.

E. How to Get Cooperation from Another Department

Think of a person in another department that you depend on to get your work done. Answer the following with "yes" or "no."

1. Is the person a friend?
2. Have you explained exactly what you need?
3. Have you asked the person for a special favor?
4. Have you asked how you may help him/her?
5. Have you issued mild threats?
6. Do you get your work done on time when the person does not cooperate?

Consider "yes" to be the correct answer for all questions.

Few people work in isolated silos. As a frustrated employee explained, "To do my job, I have to depend upon a person in another department to do her job. She does not work for me. I have no control over her. I don't think she even likes me."

If you are not satisfied with the help you currently get from a person in another department, you must change the way you approach the person. Consider the following.

Enemies Are Not Helpful

No matter the anguish the other party causes, you must try to become friendly. You cannot expect to get help from someone you treat like a lurking menace.

Change your attitude. Do not view the person as an obstacle. Put away your hurt and revenge seeking attitudes. So long as you treat people as opponents, they are not likely to be helpful.

Begin treating the targeted person as an ally. Invite him to lunch with your group. Stop by for a visit. Email helpful information. Call. Consider a token gift. Buy coffee. Caution: If your actions are phony, the person will not trust you.

Be Specific with Your Requests

Avoid nagging. Uncooperative people do not often respond to whiny, repeated requests. Avoid terms like, "as soon as you can," "when it's convenient," "as early as possible." Be specific. Be exact. For example, "Barbara, I'm winding up my project. If I can get your data by Monday, I would consider it a special favor."

Offer to Help

It is easy enough to get frustrated because we do not get what we need. But your ally in the other department needs things too. Offer to help her. Do her a favor. If the person is short of supplies, give her some of yours. Offer personal assistance with things that you do well.

Do not expect something for nothing. You may say, "It's her job," and it may be. But the odds are she has lots of responsibilities. If you want to maneuver your priority to the top of her list, pay for it by assisting in some way.

If All Else Fails, Consider Threats only as a Last Resort

OK, so you have tried everything. You are at your wit's end. Nothing has worked. Further delays, or lack of support, may jeopardize your performance.

It might be appropriate to consider a little hard ball. Consider a mild threat such as, "If you don't get me what I need, you may cause my boss to lose the account. I don't think he will like that." Or, "I'm documenting the fact that you were two weeks late with your work."

Do not bluff. If you threaten to report a person or document his failure, you must follow through. Once you threaten a person and do not act as you suggested, you have lost all leverage. Consider threats as a last resort. They can turn nasty.

Get Your Part of the Job Done

When your performance disappoints your boss, it is not very persuasive to hide behind someone else's failure with an excuse such as, "I couldn't get my work because Harry never gave me the information I needed."

Stay late. Come in early. Get help from someone else. Estimate what you do not have. Do not whine. At this point, you have to trust the higher-ups to recognize that you went to the edge of hell because of your commitment to the mission.

Chapter 11: Coach

◆

(You cannot coach slow workers into becoming record setters.)

Coaching is part teaching, part demonstrating, part encouraging, part inspiring, and part mystical. Effective leaders are good coaches. But coaching is much more than simply showing an employee how to do something. It is far more complex than merely encouraging employees.

I have observed that most coaching efforts do not pan out so well. Oh, the persons being coached may have improved, but they usually do not improve very much. And the improvement usually does not stick. After the coach turns his attention to another subject, the "improved employee" usually gravitates back to his previous marginal performance.

Leaders who learn *who* to coach and *what* to coach get far better results with much less stress to themselves and to others.

A. How I Failed as a Coach

I have talked with more than one hundred managers who have worked out plans for coaching employees' weaknesses.

To each manager, I have asked the question, "As a result of your plan, did you notice any significant and lasting improvements in the employee's weak areas?"

To date, only thirteen managers (of more than one hundred) have answered "yes "to this question. And upon a closer look, those who reported improvements indicated that improvements were marginal at best and short lasting.

I Understand that Empoloyee Development Is Important

Employee development is very important. Many authorities say that development is one of the most significant responsibilities of leaders. High-performing organizations recognize the value of "growing people."

Good companies allocate a sizable chunk of their revenues to developmental performance reviews, mentoring, career planning, and coaching as well as the more traditional training and development activities.

It is impossible to be successful unless people substantially develop their skills and abilities beyond what they brought to the company as a new hire.

Why There Are so Many Coaching Failures

I once supervised a very able employee who was excellent in dealing with clients. Her care was obvious, her empathy apparent, and she saw that clients got the services they needed.

But the employee had a flaw that distracted me terribly. All of her reports were last minute or late. She was not organized and she did not plan. Although her hair style was always neat and fashionable, her desk was a mess. She simply reacted to whatever was occurring around her.

During an early performance review, I commented, "Although you work great with our clients, I think you need to be better organized."

The employee readily agreed with my assessment and vowed to improve. I was pleased with her cooperative attitude. We established as her top goal, "... to be better organized."

Being eager to work a miracle with this willing employee, I set specific items to organize and dates to get them done. She bought a popular large planning calendar that promised to organize anyone's day, week or life. I enrolled the employee in a workshop on time management and bought her a book on how to get control of her life.

Although I reviewed the employee five more times, and talked about the need for her to become better organized dozens of times, I do not believe that she improved even five percent.

My developmental efforts with this employee failed because I focused on her weaknesses. We foolishly think that if we continuously work on employees' shortcomings, we will someday soon have a perfect, or near perfect, work group.

As researchers Marcus Buckingham and Curt Coffman report in their book, *First, Break All the Rules,* "People don't change that much. Don't waste time trying to put in what was left out."

How I Might Have Been Successful as Coach

The stark reality is that all humans are flawed. People are not perfect. In every case, something has been left out.

Successful leaders understand that they can make a lot more hay by nurturing employees' strengths than they can by flogging their weaknesses.

Yes, in working with my "disorganized employee," I would have been more successful had I bought her a book on sensitivity, enrolled her in an effective listening workshop, and encouraged her to continue responding to client requests.

Successful developers identify employees' strengths and they work to improve them. Would the world have been better off if Shakespeare had spent more time trying to improve his singing?

B. You Get Better Returns by Coaching Better Talent

I was about ten years old when I understood that I did not have musical talent. I was taking guitar lessons and doing OK. During rehearsal for an upcoming recital, Mary Ruth Young, a young lady from another group joined us on the piano.

At a break, someone asked her to play a song titled, "Under the Double Eagle." Mary Ruth said, "I don't think I've ever heard that song. Can you hum it for me?" The person hummed the song and Mary Ruth, having never before heard it, started playing it on the piano. Then she picked up a fiddle and played the song again. After that, she played it on a guitar. That's when I realized that Mary Ruth had something I did not have—musical talent.

Talent is the innate ability to do something well over and over again. Talent may result partly from very early childhood experiences, but genetics is probably the greatest carrier.

You cannot train talent! If a person has talent, coaching, training and effort will certainly cause the person to improve, usually pretty dramatically. When talent is lacking, we may still improve with coaching and training but not much.

The best leaders first screen for talent, and then invest heavily in development.

How to Tell if a Person Has Talent

All jobs, even simple ones, require talent. Not everyone can become a good musician, painter, or athlete. Similarly, not everyone can become a good welder, record keeper, report writer, receptionist, mechanic or janitor.

To determine if a person has a talent, ask four questions.

1. Is the person already pretty good at doing the task? Is the person pretty fast? Is the work accurate? Do the tasks seem as natural as breathing? If a person is pretty good with little or no training, additional training, experience, and hard work gets them even better.
2. Does the person like to do the task? Most of us like to do what we are naturally talented to do. If we just do not like doing something, the odds are, we do not have a talent for it. Training and development will not cure this ailment.
3. When you show a person something new, does the person catch on quickly? Persons who get it quickly have talent. A person who must work five times harder than others and still cannot keep up just does not have the talent to do the job.
4. Does the training stick? If three days after your expert coaching session, your employee says, "I seem to have forgotten how to do that, can you show me again?" this may be a sign of limited talent.

Suppose you supervise data input specialists. One employee can accurately input at the rate of 95 words per minute (wpm). Another can only do 25 wpm. There is a two-day workshop in Orlando that teaches the latest and greatest techniques in data input. You have enough in the budget to send one person. Who do you send?

Most people say they would send the 25 wpm person. Why? They have the most room for improvement. One of the greatest myths in training and development is, if we do something poorly, we have a lot of room for improvement.

Research shows us that you can get a ten-percent improvement in the person doing 95 wpm more quickly than you can get a ten-percent improvement in the 25 wpm person.

To succeed in developing your people, invest in coaching employees who have talent. Replace the ones who do not.

C. Discontinue Coaching Unless You See Immediate Results

Leopards do not change their spots. Zebras cannot change their stripes. And employees do not change their core work behaviors much, if at all. ˙

Slower workers will always be slower workers. Mistake-prone employees will continue to make more mistakes than others. Employees, who cannot get to work on time, even after you terminate them, will continue to be late—albeit at some other company. Whiners at age thirty will be whiners at age sixty.

Does Coaching Work?

The answer is "yes" and "no."

Yes, coaching works for employees who have underlying talents but little training or experience. Some individuals have a knack for serving customers. Some are naturals for repairing equipment. Some, from early childhood, keep meticulous, detailed records. A few have a great ear for music. Add training and experience to these natural talents and you get great performances.

No, coaching does not work when we try to significantly help no-talents. Some of us just do not cooperate very well. Some would not recognize empathy even if they could see a picture of it. Others are just not good with details. Most of us are tone deaf. The greatest voice coaches in the universe would quickly consider leaping out of a ten-story window if their futures depended on improving my singing.

The bad news is coaching does not dramatically change the behavior of employees who have no talent to begin with. The good news is you can easily tell whether a person has the talent. Just note how quickly they improve.

Employees who get it quickly, show immediate and lasting improvement, and exhibit satisfaction in improving are coachable. By contrast, those who do not ever get it the first time, have to be reminded at later periods, and do not seem to enjoy the learning process are coaching sink holes.

The Two Greatest Coaching Mistakes

The greatest coaching mistakes involve high performing employees who have disruptive attitudes. I have had the opportunity to counsel with dozens of professionals about their attitudes and how it was short circuiting their careers. In ninety percent of the cases, the professionals immediately began revealing their attitudes by arguing with the feedback. And they still did not get it.

On several occasions, I have attempted to explain to employees how their negative attitudes were affecting their careers. I have never heard from any of the troubled employees the following, "Oh, thank you for that helpful information. I was wondering what I might be doing wrong."

A second coaching mistake is to focus on employees' weak performance areas. Most employees have a combination of strengths and flaws. We can ignore their strengths easily enough. The work still gets done. Flaws scream at us louder that a fire truck siren.

Recognize, however, that most of what we call "flaws" are really areas of little or no talent. Heroic coaching efforts may get improvement but not much. If you want to help employees improve, work on their strong areas. Because they have talents in these areas, they will continue to improve.

Why Managers Persist

Why do so many managers persist in their coaching when results are disappointing? Recall that it is hard for us to change our behaviors. Some managers were born to coach. They have a talent for it. They like to do it. They consider people development important to their success.

I say "hooray" for such managers, but I advise them to "water where the flowers grow" and apply their coaching skills to employees' talented areas.

D. Do Not Invest in Personal Improvement Plans Unless You are Willing to Terminate

"What do you do about an employee who is not performing?" I asked a group of managers.

Many responded, "We set up a Personal Improvement Plan (PIP)."

A PIP resembles an informal contract between a manager and an employee.

It usually sets improvement targets and dates for achieving them. For example: (1) within 30 days, your performance level will be at the 98 percent rate, (2) I expect no complaint calls from internal customers, and (3) no unexcused absences. Failure to achieve these goals may result in disciplinary action.

"What is the purpose of your PIP?" I ask.

"To get the employee to improve," is often the response.

"What happens if the employee does not improve?"

"Well, they could be fired."

"Do you usually fire people who do not meet all of the requirements in your PIP?"

"They usually improve for awhile."

"And then their performance slips again?"

"Yes, we usually get a little improvement. Not as much as we had hoped. You are right; performance often drops off after awhile."

Most Employees on PIPs Do Not Significantly Improve

Most employees' commitment to improvement last about as long as their New Year's resolutions to lose weight.

I do agree with the PIP concept. I also understand that most marginal employees have been marginal producers for a good while. And only about one in five PIP employees get better.

Four out of five PIP employees show temporary, short-term improvements. Then, they drift back to sub-par performance.

This improvement-and-drift-back cycle may last several months—sometimes even longer. During this period, many other things happen—the employee gets a new boss, assignments change, other priorities emerge, unexpected distractions surface. The result is that the well-intended PIP just fades away without a clear conclusion. The employee does not improve and management does not fire the employee.

Do Not Establish a PIP Unless You Are Willing to Terminate

It is a fact that most PIPs do not cure marginal performances. For that reason, managers should be prepared to terminate all employees they put on PIPs who do not live up to the letter of the plan. Failure to do so results in two bad things.

One, no matter how hard you work at it, at the end of the day, a mistake-prone, slow-working, disruptive, argumentative employee is still going to be more of a liability than an asset. Managers, human resource professionals, and the company get little return on their investments of time and effort. They squander their energies which could have gone into more productive endeavors.

Two, by publicly attacking the issue of sub-par performance, other employees pay close attention to the results. Make no mistake, all employees in the area will be fully aware of any PIP in their midst. Some privately speculate on who is going to win. "Will the company actually fire him?"

If the employee does not show significant and lasting improvements and if the company does not fire the employee, the implied message is loud and clear, "We are not going to fire anybody."

What will the next manager think when faced with a poor performer? I will tell you. They will think, "I'm not going to put myself through all of the aggravation of a PIP. It won't do any good anyway."

The lesson for management is, "If you are not going to bite, you had better not bark."

E. Effective Coaches Spend a Lot of Time with High Performers

Which employees take most of your time?

Problem employees.

How many problem employees do you have?

Just a couple, thank goodness!

Why do you spend so much time with your problem employees?

I try to coach and counsel them. I want to find out why there are problems and get them fixed. I talk to them about how important it is to be at work, about making sure that they do not make careless mistakes. I stress the importance of meeting deadlines, but I spend most of my time coaching them on how to work better with others.

Have you had good success in significantly improving your problem employees?

Not really.

Do you spend a lot of time with your good employees?

Not a whole lot.

Why?

They don't really need me. They come to work, do their jobs and get along. I spend time with them in our meetings and I make sure that they know what I want done. But they just don't require much maintenance.

Many managers admit they spend more time trying to fix problem employees than they do working with good ones. This is backwards! Upside down! Everyone will be better off if you spend more time with your good performers.

Why You Should Spend more Time with Good Employees

Remember, it is your good performers who pay your bills, get you promoted and allow you to enjoy your golf game. Spend more time with them.

Learn from the good ones. Ask them to show you and others how to do things better. Ask their opinions on lots of things. Use their suggestions frequently.

Give the good performers more training. To the extent that your budget allows, send them to programs in New York, Miami or Beijing. Encourage them to visit other companies, even companies in other industries, to study their "best practices."

By all means show good employees a lot of appreciation. Visit them frequently. Buy them coffee. Take them to lunch. Recognize them privately and publicly at every opportunity. Shower them with praise. Make sure that they get recognized in your company recognition programs. Post their accomplishments in newsletters, on bulletin boards, on websites. If problem employees complain, listen politely and ignore their complaints.

I understand that some of your very good employees may have minor weaknesses. Perfection is not a human trait. For minor flaws, coach employees on how to improve, but do not overdo it. If otherwise good employees do not improve quickly, the odds are they do not have the talent to easily overcome the weakness.

Find some other way of dealing with performers' minor weaknesses or simply ignore them. Do not stubbornly focus extraordinary and time-consuming efforts on correcting minor flaws. Your odds of turning minor weaknesses into strengths are just about the same as your odds of bankrupting a Las Vegas Casino. Your time with good employees should focus on their strengths.

Finally, give the good performers good pay increases. The more recognition performers get, the higher their pay raises should be. Avoid the common practice of sprinkling your pay increases like crumbs to everyone. If your average pay increase is 3 percent, give the good ones 6 or 7 percent. Average producers may get only 2 percent. Problem employees get no increase. Do not let chronic whiners influence your merit recommendations.

F. How the Artful Use of Questions Can Be an Effective Coaching Tool

You have just promoted a high performing employee to a supervisory position. The employee is energetic, eager and talented. He also gets along well with others. Although short on experience, the rookie absorbs new information like a sponge. He is committed to the mission and is internally motivated.

You have clearly explained the key objectives of your department and the metrics you will use to measure progress. You believe the new supervisor's role and responsibilities are clear.

Take Advantage of Non Routine Decisions to Coach Employees

After experiencing mostly routine situations for the first two months, the supervisor faces a decision that is clearly not routine. The supervisor requested a meeting with you and explained, "I'm concerned about the new delivery person we've hired."

"Specifically, what is the concern?" you ask.

"I'm getting complaints from other departments that he is frequently late and can be rude."

There are two basic ways the manager can help the supervisor determine how to handle issues like this.

Traditional Coaching Suggests Solutions to Problems

The more traditional managerial response is to offer a solution to the supervisor.

For instance, "I think you need to document the exact number of late deliveries and the number of complaints you have received from other departments."

Coaching continues, "Talk to the other department heads and learn more about the situations. Then you need to write a written reprimand for the employee's file. Tell the employee that, during the next month, you expect all deliveries to be made on time. Failure to do so could result in more serious consequences."

This may be a very appropriate solution. However, the manager solved the problem for the supervisor, and in the process, lost an opportunity for leadership development. The challenge of the supervisor is to simply implement the solution of his boss. Further, suppose the solution does not work so well. It is very tempting for the supervisor to lay the blame off on his boss. After all, it was the boss's recommendation.

Consider a Socratic Coaching Approach

Although it is tempting to give solutions to inexperienced supervisors, consider asking questions to help supervisors clarify and evaluate their alternatives. For instance, "How often is the employee late? Who has complained? What are the complaints? How has the employee responded to the complaints?"

Coaching continues, "What have you done to this point? What other alternatives are you considering? What is good and bad about each alternative? What are you considering as your next step?"

Such questions prompt the supervisor to think through the situation. They force him to develop alternatives rather than merely solicit an answer from the boss.

If the manager believes that the supervisor is moving toward a bad solution, he can offer further guidance such as, "I think you may have trouble implementing that approach. Do you know whether it's consistent with our personnel policies?"

If the supervisor comes up with a reasonable solution, the manager can support him, "Sounds like a good approach to me." Because the supervisor solved his own problem, he will be even more committed to implementing his suggestions. Because the manager supported the supervisor, the supervisor will gain confidence in handling future situations.

Chapter 12: Appraise

✦

**(If I don't turn performance appraisals in on time,
someone will track me down.)**

Most managers approach the performance appraisals of their employees with about the same enthusiasm as they do a visit with their dentist. Most employees actually prefer to have formal appraisals, but many say their system is confusing.

I think managers should enjoy appraisals. Look at it this way, the manager gets a chance to sit down with staff members and tell them about all of the good things they have done the past year, and they get to discuss suggestions for getting even better.

When I am around employees and I hear them saying things like, "I'm excited about my meeting on Monday because my manager is doing my performance appraisal," I know the company has the right approach to performance appraisals.

A. Two Suggestions for Improving Performance Reviews

Nothing appears to tangle supervisors' judgments more than performance appraisals. Supervisors do them only because they have to and then they complain endlessly about how bad the process is.

"We have a forced distribution," is a common complaint. "We can only give a certain percentage of employees a high rating."

"I gave one of my employees a 'five' (the highest rating)," complained another, "and I had to write several paragraphs about why she was so good."

Still another said, "It's just easier to mark everyone 'acceptable.' No one seems to mind and you get the process done quicker."

Another supervisor admitted, "The hardest part is to be honest with an employee who is not doing the job."

Three Traditional Problems with Performance Reviews

Historically, three problems have plagued performance reviews. One, supervisors tend to inflate their ratings over time. A fifth-year supervisor, other things equal, is likely to give higher reviews in his fifth year than he did his first year.

Two, supervisors are inconsistent among themselves. Some earn a reputation as "easy graders"; others become known as "hard graders."

Three, departmental performance does not match the performance ratings. Ratings may increase every year even if performance tanks. "I know our performance is down," rationalized a manager, "but we are working harder now than we were three years ago."

Maybe the manager is right, but performance ratings should reflect results not effort.

Two Common-Sense Suggestions for Improving Reviews

I offer two suggestions for managers who do performance reviews.

Quit carping about your particular review system. It may not be perfect, but no review system is. I once, in jest, guaranteed a manager I could get his supervisors to support their current performance review system. Since an ocean tanker would not have held all of the managers' complaints, he asked me how.

My response, "Just change the system you currently have. Within six months, people will be saying, 'We liked our old system a lot better.'"

Understand the mechanics of your system and offer the best, most honest and meaningful feedback that you can. If you need to write additional notes, do so. Accept the facts that performance ratings should provide helpful feedback to your staff, and they need to be suitable for legal purposes if employees bring actions against the company.

Two, tie individual ratings to actual results. If you rate a person high on "productivity," make sure that you have the numbers to measure productivity of this individual. If you rate a person low on "attendance," have a standard for what constitutes low attendance. Is it five absences? Eight? Ten?

For the soft scales such as "teamwork" and "cooperation," bring in actual examples from the employee's behavior. For instance, "I asked for volunteers on four different occasions, and you had an excuse each time for why you could not help." Or, "In addition to your perfect attendance and accurate work, I called on you six different times for special assignments (note the occasions) and you graciously delivered every time."

No less a leader than Jack Welch, the very successful and former CEO of General Electric, says that the annual meeting for reviewing staff performances was the most important meeting of the year.

B. Use Self Appraisals to Improve Performance Feedback

"I'm not looking forward to my review with Alfred," expressed a manager. "Last year, I noted three areas of weakness that he needed to work on. Although I talked with him several times during the year, I can't see much improvement."

Sure enough, the manager was only five minutes into the review when Alfred became more defensive than swarming bees. "An unresolved debate," was how the manager characterized the result.

This situation is typical. In a survey of 1,450 managers, researcher David DeVries concluded that employees were actually more confused about their performance after their reviews than they were before.

A company, trying to reward performers, set up a merit pay system. It required a rating of "4" on a "5-point" scale to earn the pay. How many employees received "4" or higher? Ninety-nine percent! (That must have been one record-setting group.)

Self Appraisals Help Employees Understand Their Reviews

Researcher Herbert Meyer, after a series of studies, found that self appraisal methods were more helpful than the traditional top-down performance review.

Self appraisals tend to be more satisfying to both parties. They are also more likely to improve performance.

Some critics complain, "If I let my employees review themselves, they will all be rate-busters."

Three responses are in order. First, most employees score as rate-busters under the current system. Second, most employees are pretty honest when self-reporting their performance. Third, managers do not have to agree with inflated reviews.

Avoid Salary Discussions and "Grades"

I support grades in schools and universities. But self appraisals work better when they avoid grading scales. Lose the categories of "outstanding," "above average," "meets expectations," and the like.

Also avoid discussing salary during the appraisal interview. Salary discussions drown out all other feedback.

I do not mean that salary increases should be based on tenure, likeability or randomness. High performers definitely should get higher raises. Just communicate the raise at a later time.

Instructions for Conducting Self Appraisals

Basically, self appraisals should cover accomplishments, problems, and future goals.

I like to ask subordinates to prepare for the review by writing answers to such questions as:

1. What were your three major accomplishments?
2. What were you most disappointed in?
3. What problems did you experience?
4. What are your three most important goals for next period?

I like for the answers to include data. For instance, "I completed 98 percent of my projects on time." One more thing, it is far more effective to do this quarterly than annually.

The Reviewer Should Be Actively Engaged

The reviewer should not be passive. Prepare for the review by making notes on the questions also. When employees report things you agree with, let them know. If employees report things you disagree with, tell them. When you discuss goals for the next period, ensure that your priorities are on the list.

Both parties look to traditional appraisals in the same way that they look forward to a root canal. Self appraisals put the reviewer in more of a coaching and mentoring role.

C. How to Negotiate Employee Performance

It seems to me that many managers negotiate employee performances very differently than they negotiate vendor contracts. Suppose you are purchasing materials from a reliable, respected vendor and your careful research suggests that a good price for the materials would be $50,000.

Of the following three alternatives, what offer would you most likely make to the vendor: (A) $50,000? (B) $47,000? (C) $52,000?

About 80 percent of responses say they would offer (B) $47,000. Why? They want to get the best buy they can. They can still negotiate. The vendor might take $47,000. And so on.

Managers Go Soft when Negotiating Employee Performance

Take an employee performance negotiation.

Suppose one of your employees has been performing, for several weeks, at a level of performance that we will call 40. The employee has the training and the ability to be a good producer. Assume that the typical employee produces 60 and outstanding employees produce 70.

Further assume that you discussed the issue with the employee a couple of times but have seen no improvement. In your third discussion, you are trying to set a specific performance improvement goal for the employee.

The employee responds, "I've been having some problems, but I think I can get my performance to 50 by the end of the month."

How would you respond? (A) Accept the 50. You have employee buy-in. (B) Insist on 60. The employee has the ability and you have talked with him twice already. (C) Demand 70. The employee is letting the group down.

Seventy-five percent of employees select (A) 50. Twenty percent select (B) 60, and five percent choose (C) 70.

Managers Negotiate Harder when Dealing with Vendors

When negotiating with a vendor, most people try to get the vendor to do even better no matter what the level of performance. In this case, $50,000 would have been good performance, but we try to buy the supplies for $47,000.

By contrast, when negotiating with employees, most managers, in my opinion, err too far on the side of the employee. In this case, most respondents would allow a capable employee to contribute less than what the employee is capable of doing.

When buying services from the outside, managers are pretty tough. When buying skill from an employee, managers are pretty lenient, that is, they will take less for their money.

Why is this? Both vendors and employees are human. Both have a right to earn a living. Both are very vital to the success of a business. But we have much more frequent and personal contact with our employees than we do with our vendors.

I think we allow our personal knowledge of the employee to get in the way of reasonableness.

Is it reasonable to allow a capable employee to produce 33 percent less than what is typically expected? Is it fair to other employees in the group to allow one person a different performance standard? Is it fair to owners and investors to pay wages to an employee when the employee is not contributing fair value to the department?

I think the answer to all of these questions is, "No."

I do not suggest managers fire employees when performance drops by a degree or two. I certainly understand that not all employees are going to produce at exactly the same level. I am aware that the employee relationship is different from the vendor relationship.

I do suggest that in both the cases of the vendor and the employee, managers are responsible for getting fair value for dollars spent.

D. Be Aware of the Dangers Inherent in 360-Degree Performance Appraisals

A performance appraisal based on "360-degree feedback" is a method of evaluating managers by collecting information from several sources—subordinates, peers, bosses and other groups. Individuals typically complete standardized surveys on how the manager establishes plans, takes risks, manages diversity, leads, communicates, solves problems, and the like.

The intent is to provide insights from a wide variety of people who interact with the manager. The hope is to use the feedback data to help managers improve their skills and effectiveness. Companies such as Levi Strauss, PepsiCo, and Morgan Stanley have used 360-degree feedback. Some companies tie feedback results to pay increases.

While the 360-degree feedback method has its place, as with any tool, there are also dangers.

Do Not Let the Numerical Score Overshadow Actual Results

Robert, the manager of a warehouse, met or exceeded most of his performance goals for the year. Goals included such measurable items as inventory shrinkage, breakage, and on time shipments.

During his performance review, Robert's boss said, "You are the worst manager in the division."

"I don't understand," replied Robert, "I met all of my performance objectives."

"Yes, but your composite score on our 360-feedback survey is the lowest of the group."

Can you blame Robert for being confused? He accomplished what the company wanted him to do and his boss jumps on him for being a poor manager.

Do Not Focus Attention on the Weaker Areas

All managers have flaws and 360-degree surveys will surely unearth imperfections.

The logic works like this. First, identify weaknesses. Second, create a plan for overcoming the weaknesses. Third, follow up to determine if the manager improved. Eventually, all managers will overcome their weaknesses and the company will get all of the customers in the world while competitors whine and moan.

The logic seems impeccable. But it directs attention toward managers' weakest attributes. One observer commented, "It forces us to manage to our weaknesses."

The reality is that managers can better benefit their companies by improving their strengths and increasing the asset value of their contributions.

A focus on weaknesses has two major flaws: one, it is very hard for managers to overcome their weaknesses even when they try; and two; managers' strengths erode while they concern themselves with what is wrong.

Do Not Force All Managers into the Same Mold

Standardized surveys attempt to define good managers. A high score identifies effective managers. But we know that managers have differing personalities and differing styles. Companies should not—in fact, they cannot—force all of their managers to behave alike.

We also know that many real leaders possess an intangible dimension that you cannot "bottle" for others to use.

Do Not Let a Few Employees Skew the Results

"I'll rip that SOB when we get our surveys," muttered a disgruntled employee to his friend. Some employees use the survey tool to purposefully downgrade a manager who has angered them.

Managers also become aware of this, as Bertha stated, "I know that I should reprimand my tardy employee, but our surveys will be coming out next month. I don't want him to downgrade me."

Managers are responsible for making decisions that best serve the mission of the company. Some employees will sometimes disagree with the best of managers. The 360-degree feedback may allow a peeved employee to have too much sway over management decisions.

As a feedback tool, 360-degree surveys may provide useful information from a wide variety of sources. But unless evaluators are cautious in the use of the information, they may create consequences that are harmful to the company.

E. Ensure that Your Appraisal System is Legal

Unfortunately, employment discrimination claims have become about as common as a cold. And you can bet your last dollar that the company's performance appraisal system is a major part of the evidence in every case. Would your appraisal system stand up to vigorous questioning by employment attorneys?

In studies by professors Hubert Field and William Holly, appraisal systems that meet the following four standards are more likely to stand up to legal scrutiny.

Make Job Analysis a Part of Your Appraisal System

Ensure that a job analysis is a part of the appraisal system. A job analysis is a study of what it takes to perform specific jobs. It identifies job tasks and the knowledge, skills and abilities necessary to perform the job.

As one expert commented, "A reviewer must have a full understanding of what a job requires before he can effectively rate how well a person is doing the job."

Train Managers to Give Behavior-Oriented Appraisals

Appraisals should evaluate employee behaviors, not traits. You can see employee behaviors with your eyes, for example: attendance, mistakes, on time completion, safety procedures, and cooperation.

It is effective to evaluate, and legally defensible, to judge people on how consistently they perform certain behaviors. Traits are things that you cannot see but may assume about an employee, for example: intelligence, attitude, values, and commitment.

Avoid evaluating traits. Judgments are far too subjective and cannot be proven. For example, do not rate employees on attitudes. We have about as good a chance of seeing our fairy godmother as we have of seeing an attitude.

When supervisors report that employees have a bad attitude, I ask, "How do you know?" Typical responses are: "Misses too much work." "Refuses to help others." "Refuses job assignments." "Complains about everything." "Will not go along with changes." "Makes too many mistakes."

All of these examples are behaviors and are appropriate to be part of the appraisal system. We may infer that employees have bad attitudes by how they behave, but it is much more objective to evaluate the behaviors.

Provide Written Instructions for Appraisers

Provide written instructions on how to complete the appraisal process. Instructions should include suggestions for using the rating form and definitions of what is meant by different ratings.

For instance, "What are the performance differences between excellent, satisfactory, and unacceptable?" Experts should also provide training for those responsible for conducting the appraisals.

Provide Effective Feedback to Employees

Supervisors need to meet individually with each employee to provide feedback on the ratings. Tell employees why they received certain ratings. Give examples. Refer to performance records such as measurements of work volume, errors and missed work.

When discussing a behavior such as "cooperation," give specific examples of when the employee cooperated effectively or when an employee had an opportunity to cooperate but did not.

Give examples of what the employee can do to improve. Talk about what you expect the employee to do in the future. Be specific and encouraging. Do not dwell on employees' weaknesses. Simply note them, give examples of why you think they are weaknesses and offer suggestions for improvement.

Above all, do not argue with employees about a rating. If an employee wishes to debate a point after you have given a clear explanation, say something like, "I understand your comment. On this issue, we simply have a difference of opinion."

There are no perfect systems. Surveys reveal that about three out of four supervisors and employees are dissatisfied with their current systems. If your appraisal system meets the four standards described above, it is probably pretty effective.

Chapter 13: Change

✦

(Give up on the idea that people "just don't like change.")

"How are things going?" I asked a manager.

"Very hectic," he responded. "Since the first of the year, we have been bought by another company, my whole division has been restructured, I've had three different offices and two new assistants, we are trying to implement a new software system, and I have a new boss. I'll be so glad when things return to normal!"

What is wrong with this statement? What's wrong is that change is normal. Or at least, it is close to normal. All organizations experience change constantly. The challenge is not how to get through a change. The challenge is how to remain effective during constant change. This section offers suggestions for leading employees during continuous change and maintaining some semblance of sanity in the process.

A. I Think Most People Actually Like Changes

I do not understand why there is so much mystery about change. On the one hand, managers think that people resist change like it was a medieval curse.

On the other hand, employees want a lot of things to be different. "We need better computers." "We need to improve communication." "Our product line is becoming outdated." "I do not like our performance review form." "Our information system is seriously flawed." "I wish I had a new boss."

Something is amiss here. Both managers and employees want change. And both are absolutely convinced that their ideas for change would help their company.

[157]

I have thought about this a lot. Here is what I think…

Accept the Fact that Employees like the Concept of Change

Employees like change. They seek change. If change does not occur, employees get grumpy.

Further, managers get a free ride when they say, "People naturally resist change."

Translation—"I cannot do anything about the problem. If people resist change, then it is not my fault that the new 'whatever' is not working well."

I think we have allowed managers an "easy out" by accepting the myth that people naturally resist change. We do not hold them accountable when employees stubbornly resist the new way. Thus, we hear some version of the phrase, "People don't like change," as an excuse.

The Initiative to Change Comes from All Directions

Organizational changes come primarily from four sources.

Employees bring about some changes. Employees initiate changes, when given the freedom and support, quite often. Ironically, employees so strongly want to alter methods and procedures that managers put in bureaucratic regulations to ensure that procedures remain the same.

Managers require some changes. Forward thinking managers make a lot of changes in their departments. Most such changes are how things will be done; for example, processes, procedures, forms.

Managers and employees jointly push for change. Company leaders ask several managers to help design a change, allowing subordinate managers to participate in the change decisions.

Such changes are usually strategic and complex. They impact many departments. Examples include: information technology, addition or deletion of products or services, promotional programs, distribution strategies and the like.

External agencies mandate some changes. Mandated changes come from above—frequently they are imposed by outside sources such as a governmental agency.

Managers have little or no say-so in the design of these changes. They simply are told, "Beginning on the first of the month, you will be required to..."

Execute Changes with Confident Leadership

Most problems arise with mandated and manager-participating changes. Since there is not room for negotiation in mandated changes, education is crucial. Managers fare better when they carefully explain to employees the "why" of the change. Sympathetic listening can also benefit.

Managers should avoid allowing employees to think that they can influence a mandated change by simply howling loudly. Rather, establish firm deadlines and place energy on how to make adjustments to accommodate the new way.

When managers get to participate in the design of a change, they should also seek input from their staff members. Educate staff members about alternatives and let them also help create the change. Ask questions, hold meetings, and offer drafts and prototypes.

Understand, however, that when you get staff involvement, there will likely be disagreements. Listen to opposing views, try to reconcile the differences; but in the final analysis, you must contribute your opinions to the group that is charged with directing the change.

It is normal for there to be some level of disgruntlement over the change. Even when people get to participate in the change, some will still whine. Criticism about the new way does not necessarily mean that people are resisting. Calm your mind by understanding that some level of criticism is normal no matter how well the change works.

B. Suggestions for Making Very Unpopular Changes

I understand that employees may sometimes make the most stubborn of mules seem like cooperative team players. Just try to undo what employees have come to accept as their "rights."

For instance, one firm had been very lax enforcing attendance policies. Employees thought it was their right to take a day off now and then.

A new manager came on board. After looking at attendance figures, the new person proclaimed, "Absenteeism is out of control." He began enforcing attendance policies.

In another company, employees commonly said, "I think I'll take a couple of days of sick leave next week," to do whatever. Sick leave had morphed into vacation time.

Still, another example. For more than ten years, employees had been working a traditional Monday-through-Friday workweek. To reduce costs, management began rotating schedules. Now employees had to take turns working weekends and, heaven forbid, evenings.

One more. Competitive pressures forced management to look at all costs. Fringe benefits had escalated for several years. Management said, "We have to cut our benefit package."

In all of these cases, employees railed against the changes. People were outraged. And in all cases, leadership bemoaned the notion that "people just don't like change."

It is not that people, "just do not like change." True, people balked in these examples, but not because they did not like change. They fought the changes because management took away some employee "rights," as in when I can take days off or how much I have to pay out of my pocket for a root canal.

By the way, you will also get resistance when you replace people with technology, freeze pay increases, or lay off employees.

Leaders sometimes must, and should, make changes that alter work traditions and culture. In some cases, lax leaders allowed inefficient practices to become part of the tradition. When the group gets a new leader or when competitive conditions change, some inefficiencies become glaring.

Make the unpopular changes when they are required and consider the following:

1. **Accept this fact.** Employees are not going to like it. Do not waste time hiring consultants to look for miraculous approaches. Most employees are not going to embrace loss of freedoms, security or money.
2. **Lay out the cold, hard facts.** Show people the numbers—rising costs, competitive inroads, shrinking profits, lost opportunities, diminishing customers, compliance issues. Facts may not dull the pain, but they can show that it is not personal.
3. **Do listen to employee input.** Employee arguments about the change being "unfair" or "unjust" may not be persuasive. But occasionally,

employees do offer helpful insights. If employees offer better alternatives, accept them.

4. **Lay out hard and fast timeline for making the changes.** Tell people exactly what is going to happen and when it will happen. I know that complicated situations make this suggestion hard to implement, but it is important to take uncertainty out of the equation.

5. **Expect some people to get upset.** Understand that you may have to reprimand, write-up, or otherwise discipline a few employees. Expect some to quit.

The idea is to get through the storm quickly and stay focused on the mission. There is no better salve for disconcerted employees than to share in the rewards of improved company performance.

C. Execute Change by Reducing the Causes for Resistance

I do not like to lose money. I do not like to be inconvenienced. Failure and disappointments are not high on my list of preferred things. You can also add threats, uncertainty, bad surprises and fear to this list.

But this does not mean that I oppose change. I like to get a new car (actually a new truck), and I like to try different foods. A new pup is nice as are new vegetables in the spring garden. I like to go to different places and see first-time things.

Most people embrace change. If this were not true, our daily lives could not absorb the constant barrage of change we experience. Remember when you manually rolled down the window in your automobile and stuck your arm out the window to signal a left turn?

Recall when the starter was on the dashboard? Remember when you had to hand-crank the engine? Punched cards for computers? Ten-key adding machines? Life before cell phones, smart phones, iPads? Life before telephones, for that matter? Change is a way of life and we seek it, both in our personal and in our work lives.

When People Resist Change, Find out Why

"But, isn't it true that people do resist changes in their work life," you say?

It is true that people resist a few things that accompany some changes.

People do not like layoffs, loss of income, inconvenience, fear or threats. I consider this to be a normal and rational response.

When implementing changes, it is important to identify worries and concerns that people may have. And it does not matter if the fears are perceived or actual.

Through meetings, discussions, open communications and, most of all, a past history of integrity, provide information that will allow people to be confident that they can succeed. Put simply, when considering any change, there are forces driving the change (reasons why) and forces that may cause resistance (costs and fears).

Most change efforts focus on why the change is desirable—quicker, more accurate, lower costs, better service and on and on. We pay scant attention to employee worries about job security, ability to learn the new way, loss of income and the like.

When leaders work to make employees feel safe and secure, employees will actually push for changes. They will initiate demand for new technology, products/services, streamlined procedures, tools and processes.

I understand that some changes do result in loss of income (layoffs), inconveniences (schedule change), or threats (experimental technology). I also understand that these may be necessary for future growth and success.

When the change does cause a hardship on a few employees, it is better to make the change quickly. Expect some complaining, but implement firm deadlines. Do not waste a lot of time trying to get buy-in. You will not be able to get people to buy-in to changes that truly do carry threats to their economic well-being.

D. Do Not Even Try to Get Buy-in When Managing Change

"When making a change, I try to get buy-in." explained a leader.

But another leader commented, "I think the most important way to manage change is to get people on your team who understand that change is just a way of life."

How Some Managers Strive for Buy-In

"What does buy-in mean?" I asked a change agent.

"It means that people support your position. They understand the need for the change."

"How do you go about getting buy-in?"

"When there is a need for change, I discuss it with my staff. I ask for their input. We discuss our ideas and eventually come to some agreement."

"Does everyone agree every time?"

"No, not every time. Usually, most will agree, eventually. I sometimes modify my position if that is what it takes to get agreement."

"Did I hear you say that you may go along with the majority view, even if it is different from what you think should be done?"

"If you want to get buy-in, you may have to."

How to Lead Change without Settling for Buy-In

Another leader said to me, "I don't worry about getting buy-in. I've hired people who understand that changes are necessary."

"Do you discuss proposed changes with your staff?"

"Of course. I make suggestions and we discuss them. Sometimes a staff member may have a better idea. I'm open to it. If it really is a better idea, I'll accept it. Sometimes our discussions get a little heated."

"What happens when some do not agree with your proposals?"

"At the end of the day, they understand that we all have to be on the same page. I expect them to execute the change whether they agree with it or not—and they do. If people have an opportunity to fully argue their positions, even if they lose the argument, they can still support the change."

Make the Right Decision without Worrying about Buy-In

Both approaches come to an agreement on what changes will be made. But there are subtle but meaningful differences in the two approaches.

A disadvantage of buy-in is that the process feeds a culture of majority rule. Dissident staff members become more empowered. Outliers recruit others to their cause and politic to overcome their leader's proposed change.

Because buy-in is such a strong motive of leaders using this approach, they are more likely to modify their positions just so they can get agreement (spelled buy-in). While such leaders may get their buy-in, the path they have chosen may not be the best for the company.

The buy-in approach often takes longer. Opponents to change can delay changes they disagree with by strategizing in the hallways and filibustering during meetings. Leaders, not so focused on buy-in, are more likely to strive for the best decision. Because they hold their ground better than buy-in leaders, they are more likely to end up with stronger, more effective changes.

Further, my experiences show that the stronger leaders, contrary to popular view, get better commitment from their followers. Followers of buy-in leaders often continue to negotiate decisions longer after the decisions have been made. Followers of the stronger managers are more likely to accept the decision as the last word, resulting in a greater focus on execution.

E. How to Respond to Changes When You Are Lukewarm about Them

"My staff and I worked out some changes so that we could achieve a three-percent increase in productivity," explained a middle manager. "But when I met with my vice president, he thought we could get five percent."

"Did the vice president provide any data? Offer any suggestions?" I asked.

"Yes, he had a lot of information, even had some data we didn't have. And he gave pretty good reasons for his position."

"What did you finally agree upon as the target?"

"Five percent, of course."

"So what is the problem?"

"When I went back to my staff, some felt like I had sold them out."

"How did you respond?"

"I tried to explain why the vice president thought we could get five percent, but I don't think I was persuasive."

Sometimes you have to execute decisions that differ from your original position. What do you do?

Understand that Opposing a Boss's Change is "Passing the Buck"

You can go back to your group with, "Sorry, but I just couldn't make the sale. They are insisting that we get five percent. I don't agree with it but it's what they want."

Subordinates get the message that you do not really expect them to achieve the goal. They go about business as usual and assume that not much has changed.

You can do this, but don't. Such an approach is "passing the buck," pure and simple. You may get temporary relief from staff pressure, but employees do not respect this approach. They see you as selling out to the home office and not providing leadership. Not to mention, you are really being disloyal to your upper level leaders.

If You Try for Middle Ground, You are Not Leading

You can go back to your staff and state the reasons why leadership made the decision.

In a detached way, you can objectively convey the pros and cons of the decision, fully explain upper management's rationale, and do it clearly but not convincingly. The implication is that upper management has the right to make the call, and this is the call they made.

Staff members understand that you do not "own" the change. All realize that they work for higher-level managers. Employees begrudgingly set about to execute the decision, but as unwilling participants, wondering if this is really the job for them. Such an approach is better than direct opposition but not much. You are still not leading.

It is More Effective to Commit to the Change

"I went into the planning discussions confident of my position," explained a manager.

"The boss had a different view. We had an intense discussion. The boss won."

"What did you do?" I asked.

"I thought, 'Maybe the boss knows something I don't.' If he thinks we can do it, maybe we can. Anyway, I'm part of leadership. I believe that I need to get on board or find another job."

The manager explained further, "When I had the meeting with my staff, I reviewed the data the boss and I discussed. And then I said, 'I know we planned a little differently, but I believe we can do this. I want you to tell your employees that this is my expectation. It is not the vice-president's, nor the president's, nor the board's expectation. It is my expectation.'"

The manager also said to his staff, "I want you to tell your people that it is your expectation. We are doing this because we think it is the right business decision. And if you do not believe that it is the right business decision, then our meeting is not over yet."

This is leadership. Do the right thing for the business. Be loyal to the management team. Believe in your abilities to get the job done and pass this along to your people.

F. Five Steps for Overcoming Resistance to Merger-Related Changes

Some wit remarked that the three most common lies are, "The check is in the mail," "What a beautiful baby," and "There will be no changes after the merger."

Not only will there be changes after the merger, there were probably many changes before the merger. It is a fact; organizations that do not change do not survive. Mergers in particular, usually spawn far-reaching systematic changes.

Company leaders usually want their communication and data gathering and sorting systems to use the same software. Translation, "All divisions will use the same information technology software." Human Relations policies need to be consistent across divisions. Accounting systems need to conform to consistent formats.

Of course, mergers may initiate other changes such as new managers, new policies, new products, and new territories. Most employees understand that they have to adapt to changes.

I think it reasonable to assume the following: (1) employees accept change better when they understand it, (2) it is normal for people to resist changes that threaten them, and (3) no matter how well you execute the change, a small percentage will whine like a cat with its tail caught.

Consider the following when implementing merger-related changes.

Communicate! Communicate! Communicate!

Engage all internal communication resources to tell people about the changes. Develop a traveling road show and get the executives out to personally explain. Publish dates and deadlines. Explain in advance what is going to happen. Tell why.

If there are uncertainties, explain the probabilities. View communication as an educational program. Push the information to all nooks and crannies of the organization. Be honest. Do not sugarcoat the bad news. Make very few outright promises. Keep every single promise that you make. Implore employees to anticipate the adventure.

Try to Involve People Who Are Impacted by the Changes

When possible, involve people. Ask for suggestions. I understand that people may not get to decide whether they want to make a given change, but you might ask them for suggestions on how best to adapt to the change.

Hold meetings with departments. Answer questions fully. Listen, with an open mind, to opinions. Do not pretend to negotiate changes that are non-negotiable.

Find Ways to Support Your Employees

It is natural for people to fear the unknown. Be patient when stress levels elevate. Offer realistic encouragement. Offer training when necessary. Make "experts" available to help transcend the rough spots. Budget for necessary materials, tools and equipment. Help facilitate problem-solving sessions. Stay positive.

Consider Compromises where Practical

It is impossible to anticipate all possible hurdles presented by significant changes. A compromise now and then may be in order. It may be OK to occasionally extend a deadline. Maybe just a little more budget would help a lot. It could be that eighty percent of implementation is still pretty effective.

Be careful here. Do not compromise simply because performances or schedules are behind plan. Just consider a compromise, now and again.

Use Coercion as a Last Resort

If you fully engage the first four steps, most people will get on board pretty quickly. For the few who do not make an honest effort to absorb the changes, make their choices clear.

For instance, "We do require that all people comply with the new recording and reporting practices. Your decision is not whether you want to do it, but whether you want to remain a part of the team."

I personally think some leaders spend too much time fretting about how to get people to accept changes. Tell people what is required. Show them how to do it. Listen to suggestions. Answer questions honestly. Provide necessary materials and resources. Do not lose too much sleep worrying about the very few who no longer want to be a part of the team.

Chapter 14: Conflict

$\blacklozenge$

(Even the most compatible people will sometimes disagree.)

Conflict is simply a disagreement, as "I know you think we should paint it green, but I think customers will like it better if it is blue." Or, "I would like Mexican food. You want Chinese food?"

Most disagreements at the workplace are rather mild. A good discussion between the disagreeing parties usually settles the matter without acrimonious accusations or raised voices. A few disagreements evolve into hurtful, relationship-destroying episodes. Most leaders welcome disagreements and even passionate debates over the issues. But harsh and lasting conflicts among parties, between departments, and within a team can severely damage effectiveness.

A. Avoid Typical, Leader-Generated Conflicts

"I'm so mad I could spit," exclaimed a frustrated division manager. "We just had a big order go 'south' with a major customer. How do we respond? My production guy and my sales guy are acting like third-graders blaming each other for a broken window pane."

At a meeting to remedy the late-delivery problem, the sales manager opened with, "Why can't you get your people to do their jobs, so that I can get orders to my clients on time?"

"Why don't you quit promising clients delivery times that are impossible to meet?" countered the production manager.

It is in the interest of all to make the customer happy. Why do they not see this? Why do people in the same company want to poke each other's eyes out when they would be better off cooperating to make customers happy and make more profits?

Such dilemmas occur between mature and educated people because leaders stress "A" while rewarding "B." The division manager stressed *cooperation* but rewarded *competition*.

The company incentive system paid bonuses to sales people for total sales. To get his incentive, the production manager had to keep production costs and scrap rates under control. The managers focused on their bonuses even if it meant competing with each other.

Humans are smart. No matter what we say, most people respond to what we reward. Unfortunately, my observations reveal many conflicts between what leaders stress and what they reward.

Quality Versus Schedule

Every leader stresses quality work. Quality is the subject of many meetings. It is the topic of considerable training. Quality posters adorn office and plant walls. Mission statements inevitably make statements supporting "quality."

But in most companies scheduling is king. On-time shipments are critical. Many an operator has said, "If we spent just a little more time on this, we could get it right."

And many an operator has felt the wrath of leadership when the shipment left a few days late. As a seasoned employee explained, "If there is a conflict between making the schedule and improving the quality, I know I'm going to ship on time."

Commitment to Mission Versus Personal Loyalty

All leaders stress commitment to the mission, to the goals, to customers, to employees, and even to vendors.

Too many leaders reward personal loyalty. Although it is seldom spoken, insightful employees know that it is better to suffer through problems with vendors and even customers than to do anything that would make the boss look bad.

Further, employees who develop the knack of making their bosses look good, no matter what, are candidates to receive unearned rewards from same.

Communication Versus Secrets

Communication is an issue. Always has been. Always will be. All companies stress communication. "I'll be candid with you," explains the leader. "I want you to be open with me. I want to improve communication."

I have seen countless leaders stress their desire and commitment to good communications.

I have seen too many of those same leaders, at future meetings on sensitive topics, close the meeting with, "Let's keep the subject of these discussions in the room until we have had a chance to talk about this again."

Heaven help the employee who suggests, "My people are really interested in this issue. I think the rumors are just going to get worse if we don't tell them what we are thinking." And woe be it unto the subordinate who gets caught revealing the topic to employees.

Actually, we desire both competition and cooperation, quality and on-time shipments, mission and personal loyalties, openness and trusting others with secrets.

But these topics often fight with each other. Employees figure out quickly which side of the issue we value most. It is the side we reward, not necessarily the side we stress.

B. What is Your Comfortable Style for Dealing with Conflicts?

Conflicts are disagreements. Conflicts in organizations occur around four major themes:

People disagree over what should be done; how something should be done; who should do it; or the amount of rewards they should receive for doing something.

Five Styles for Approaching Conflict

Most people develop favorite ways of doing things and this includes how they approach conflicts. Suppose a manager and an employee disagree over a merit pay increase. The manager recommends a three-percent increase; the employee believes that he deserves six percent. Professors Thomas and Kilman suggest five different ways that we may approach conflicts.

1 *Win-Lose (aggressive)*

The manager insists that she is right and the employee is wrong. "I've evaluated your work objectively. You only deserve three percent and that is what you are going to get."

2. *Lose-Win (permissive)*

The manager gives in. "Well, I tend to disagree, but you probably have more insight into this than I do. I'll change my recommendation to six percent."

3. *Compromise (split the difference)*

The manager gives a little. "I am not in full agreement that you should receive six percent, but I'm willing to compromise and recommend four-and-a half percent."

4. *Lose-Lose (avoid)*

The manager avoids making a decision. "I'm not sure that I'm right and I'm not sure that you are right. I need some more time on this."

5. *Win-Win (problem solver)*

The manager seeks alternatives that allow both parties to get what they need. "I understand that you desire a higher pay increase. Let's discuss some alternatives that would result in a higher performance for me and a pay increase for you."

Few of us would use the same style of conflict resolution to all situations. Most of us have some flexibility, but the odds are that we also have more comfort with some of these approaches than we do with others.

Recall several recent conflicts? What were you most comfortable doing? Insisting on your way? Giving in? Compromising? Avoiding the issue? Solving the problem?

Be Flexible when Dealing with Others

Since it is almost impossible to get the other party to change his conflict resolution style during a disagreement, it is important for you to consider selecting a style (even though it may not be your favorite) that works.

Aggressor. When the other party uses an aggressive style, it is effective for you to become more of an aggressor. You may eventually, after much bluffing and threatening, be able to reach a compromise agreement, but it will take you longer than you desired. It is hard for aggressors to trust nonaggressive individuals when disagreeing. They simply do not understand them.

Permissive. Even when a permissive person disagrees with you, they will not make an issue out of it. They will simply accept your position. You may want to be careful that you do not take undue advantage of the permissive person and cause them to avoid you in the future.

Compromiser. Since compromisers are willing to "give a little," they will usually ask for a little more than they think they truly deserve. Thus, if you ask for a little more than you think is fair for you, you can usually reach an equitable agreement in a short time.

Avoider. It is very hard to know when an avoider disagrees with you because they do not like to express their differences.

Problem Solver. This is the easiest person to work with when there is a disagreement. Simply be open, honest and direct in your dealings with this person. Take the time to understand what she wants. Explore alternatives together to seek an answer that is satisfactory to both of you.

Conflicts can actually be beneficial. Disagreements can produce better ideas of what and how to do things. It is not necessary to prevent conflicts. It is helpful to resolve them professionally and quickly.

C. How to Handle Conflicts with Your Boss

"I am very frustrated," reported a supervisor. "My department manager has rearranged the work schedules of our employees to try to get more coverage during peak customer contact periods."

The supervisor continued to explain that the department manager's decision would destroy employee morale in her department. Some employees would have to work Saturdays and others would have days off during the week. The supervisor further commented, "I don't know why people forget what it is like when they get promoted to desk jobs."

It is Understandable that We may Disagree with Our Bosses

It is not necessary for subordinate managers to fully agree with their bosses. In fact, it is unrealistic to think that confident, well-trained staffs believe that their bosses always see the future perfectly through crystal balls.

The few people (probably about 10 percent) who agree with their managers all of the time may not be completely honest. We degrade these folks with labels such as: brown noses, yes-persons, suck-ups and worse.

I believe that highly committed subordinates agree with bosses about one-third of the time.

This can be very frustrating to both the bosses and subordinates. It seems that confident managers assume that since both they and their boss are clear-headed and smart, it follows that they should agree on all things important.

What to Do about Disagreements with Your Boss?

When disagreements occur, supervisors have a tendency to take them too personally and they get their feelings hurt. As one supervisor said, "I felt like I was betrayed." It is much better to consider the disagreements as normal and consider tactics such as:

- Discuss with the boss. Although the person we have disagreed with is probably the last person that we wish to talk with, he (she) should be the first person we talk with. Explain your concerns. Show data to support your view. Suggest alternatives.

- Keep an open mind. Try hard to see the issues from the higher managers' perspective. Because of their responsibilities, they may view things differently. And they have access to different information. As one cooperative subordinate put it, "When I disagree with the boss, I figure that there is a possibility that he just might know something that I do not."

- Accept the decision. Even if you disagree, it is better to accept the decision. Try to execute the decision as well as you can. To use a military phrase, "salute and execute." Organizational effectiveness requires coordination. Those managers who insist on doing it their way in spite of what their boss says seal their own doom. The organization will not do so well either.

- Avoid complaining. Do not opine to your subordinates, "I don't like this decision any better than you do, but they said we have to do it so we have to do it." Such buck passing causes your staff to disregard your leadership and it does not serve the mission either. It is not effective for managers who disagree with their bosses to start "doing their own thing."

- Do not "second guess." In some cases, the future will show that you were correct and your boss made a mistake. It is understandable that we want to shout, "I told you so. If you had listened to me, this would not have happened." Rather, maintain your commitment and offer alternatives that you think could help get the group out of the predicament they are in.

Most can support higher-up decisions with which they agree. True professionals learn how to make their superiors' decisions work when they disagree.

D. How to Address Conflicts Brought about by a Multigenerational Workforce

"The younger people today are just not loyal." "Generation Xers don't trust the system." "There is less respect for authority today." "Our younger employees will quit and walk down the street and take another job." "Employees today get stressed out if they have to work a 40-hour week." And on and on. We have all heard, or made, similar comments.

Social observers like to label and categorize these differences and have come up with descriptions such as:

Traditionals. Born before 1945, shaped by military experiences and a culture with more traditional values, strong work ethic, loyalty, more comfortable with top-down management, grew up without computers and cell phones.

Baby Boomers. Born between 1946 and 1964, pretty traditional, optimistic, enjoy perks (parking space, titles), embrace long term rewards like profit-sharing, concerned about work-life balance, like to socialize at conventions, large network group, anxious about GenXers.

Generation X. Born between 1965 and 1980, enjoy freedom and work flexibility, many have dependent children, less trusting, more skeptical, seek portable benefits, informal, not as impressed with titles.

Generation Y (Nexters). Born after 1980, like flexible working times, more likely to be absent and tardy, like work-at-home technology, see any job as short-term, expect to experience four or five different careers, want to make a difference, question authority, and want to have multiple choices.

I understand that different age groups look at the world differently. Older people always have different interests than younger people. Sixty year-olders talk more about their golf game, travel to Europe, visiting the grandchildren and retiring while lamenting that "…the world is going to hell." Twenty-year olders talk about computers, video games, social parties, freedom to pursue off-the-job interests, while complaining that "…the old folks just don't get it."

I think this is more of a function of age than being shaped by the events of the 1960s or 1980s. I have an acquaintance who, at the age of 26, canceled a meeting with an important client to run a marathon. The same person, 30 years later, canceled a hunting trip with his buddies to conduct company business. Marriage, children, and debt have a way of changing our perspective.

At every decade, younger people always miss more work, have broader outside interests, and seem less loyal to a particular organization. Older employees, on average, always register more job satisfaction, loyalty to the company, and commitment to the mission. This has been true for at least a dozen decades, probably longer.

I believe managers make mistakes by significantly altering their policies for different age groups. It is just not effective to have different practices for newer and younger employees than for more experienced and older employees.

I like to keep things simple. Expect all employees to support your mission. Hold all persons accountable for their work performances. Avoid liberalizing attendance policies to accommodate a few. Reward all according to their contributions. Hold 20-year-olders and 60-year-olders to the same standards.

I'm not insightful enough to devise policies, practices and procedures that can be different for each age group and still be fair to all. I expect traditional employees to use computers and I expect Nexters to come to work on time. I hope this does not mean "… that I just don't get it."

E. A Survival Guide for Office Politics

"The problem with this company," complained a frustrated employee, "is that there is too much politics involved."

"Can you give me an example?" I asked.

"Oh, you know," he said. "If you want to get appreciated, you have to support the boss's pet projects. I'm not a suck up, I'll tell you that!"

This employee believed that leaders in the organization were treating him like an unwelcome guest because he did not play the right brand of politics.

The boss, though, had a different view. His analysis of the employee was, "His performance is marginal and he has a bad attitude."

Just what is Office Politics?

Office politics represent attempts to curry support based on personal relationships rather than on merit. For instance, a manager said to a peer, "You know, I've supported you on your last two budget requests. Now, I really need your support for my request."

People refer to this political behavior as "call in your chits," "collecting on favors," or "he owes me one." The attempt to gain favor based on relationships appears in many places—promotions, pay increases, budget allocations, job assignments, support for projects.

Political Behavior Occurs in all Organizations

Do office politics exist in all organizations? Yes, in reality, political behaviors comprise a part of the human condition. And since all organizations employ humans, office politics are alive and well.

While you cannot eliminate politics, in my opinion, you can reduce the impact of politics. Leaders who discourage politics do an excellent job of identifying specific performance expectations. Further, nonpolitical leaders collect good data that show whether people are producing to expectations. This approach reduces the impact of being dazzled by astute politicians.

What You Need to Do to Survive Office Politics

Most successful leaders were excellent performers. They showed up for work, wrestled problems to the ground and got the job done. On the performance scale, they were among the best. Yet, many top performers do not rise rapidly in their career paths. Success, in addition to good performance, requires mastering the politics of the organization.

Here are the guidelines for improving your organizational politics.

1. Put the organizational vision first. As corny as it sounds, it is good politics to publicly support the organizational vision.
2. Support your boss. Many subordinates seem to think that all bosses are blubbering idiots. But good politics calls for you to be an ardent booster

of your boss's ideas. Yes, you can disagree with your boss on occasion, but if you disagree more than 20-30 percent of the time, you may need to reevaluate your position.

3. Pick up on the unspoken company values. Some companies expect employees to be active in the community. Others expect people to show up an hour early for work; be an active participant in the annual party; talk about sports; dress up for work; join the Chamber of Commerce; play in the annual golf tournament; donate to charities and so on. True, these activities may have little to do with your actual performance, but if they are a part of the organizational culture, they become important to your career.

To be good at office politics does not mean that you have to sacrifice your principles or partake in unseemly deals or develop your "brown-nosing" skill to a high art.

Good politics is often as simple as doing a good job and supporting the values of the organization. And if you have a reputation of "being good at politics," this probably means that you really are not.

Chapter 15: Negotiate
✦
(In reality, everything is potentially negotiable.)

We naturally think about negotiating with the dealer when we buy an automobile. We also negotiate with the seller when we buy a house. Management negotiates with labor unions on contracts. Buyers negotiate with vendors. Sellers negotiate with customers.

Beyond these more obvious negotiation examples, managers and employees engage daily in multiple other negotiations. "Can you work overtime this weekend?" "Will you be able to complete the job by Thursday?" "Will you support me for the promotion?" "We need to increase our output by at least ten percent." "I'd like to schedule my vacation in June."

Negotiation is the process of working out disagreements. It includes many more instances than haggling over the price of an automobile. We typically classify mergers, purchase-vendor relationships, and labor management contracts as points for negotiation.

But leaders also negotiate with subordinates about vision, goals, performance, budgets, standards, policies and so on. Negotiation, broadly defined, is an exchange of something of value between two or more parties with the intent of bettering both parties.

A. Does Your Negotiating Style Tend toward Cooperation or Competition?

Although we may not think so, negotiated agreements are almost as common as the flu. When you negotiate with another person, which of the following best describes your style?

A. I try to get what is best for me and the other party is trying to get what is best for her. I'll start with a higher price (tighter deadline, firmer policy, etc.) with the understanding that I can eventually "give a little" to make the deal if I need to.

B. My primary effort is to get a solution that is reasonable for me. My "first offer" represents what I really think is fair. I realize that I leave little or no room to bargain. I think it is important for the other party to also benefit from our agreement.

C. It is important to maintain a good relationship. I want to avoid upsetting the other party and will often do more than my share to avoid rupturing the association.

While we may vary our approach with the situation, most leaders favor one of the following three approaches.

Competitive Negotiators Try to Win

Competitive negotiations are contests. Each side tries to best the other. Negotiators use bluff and bluster. They start high. Only after much moaning and groaning do they come off their "first offer."

"My purpose is to get the best agreement that I can for my department," explained a competitive negotiator. "My company does not pay me to look out for the other party's best interest."

Cooperative Negotiators Try to be a Partner

Cooperative negotiators see the "other person" as a partner. "I'm trying to get a reasonable and fair deal," explained a cooperative negotiator. "I believe if I help him get what he needs, he'll cooperate to help me get what I need; and we'll both 'win.'"

Soft Negotiators Emphasize the Relationship

Negotiators, whose primary purpose is to preserve the relationship, are willing to do more than their share. That is, they may pay a little too much money, allow employees to miss too much work, or work for less pay than their value to the organization.

Which Style Works Better?

Authorities proclaim, and research supports, "negotiate as partners" as the most effective negotiation style. Think about it. All negotiators try for reasonable results. There is an atmosphere of trust and openness. In fact, such parties usually do not describe their efforts as negotiations. Rather, they say, "There was little to negotiate. We simply came to an agreement on what to do."

But, like the tango, it takes two to negotiate as partners. When one party wishes to cooperate (partner) and the other acts as an adversary (competitor), partnering negotiations break down. As trite as it sounds, for repeated success in negotiations, both parties must benefit.

B. How to Deal with Aggressive Negotiators

"I've just bought a new car!" exclaims your friend.

Can you guess the next phrase that is sure to spill from your friend's mouth?

Sure you can, "I got a really good deal." Your friend implies that he/she cleverly made the dealer look like a sock puppet and bought the car two standard deviations below market value.

I fail to understand why intelligent people, who buy a car every four or five years, think they can out-negotiate a dealer who may sell dozens of cars a day. The likely answer is, "We really do not know very much about negotiation."

When dealing with competitive negotiators, it may be necessary to compete. Eventually, competitive negotiators can seek the "middle ground" and reach a compromise agreement, which will likely be fair to both parties. Competitive negotiations do work. They just take too long, cost too much, and utilize too much staff energy.

As a vendor explained, "I have a customer who always insists on haggling over the price. I simply add about 10 percent to his price. We exchange messages, do our little dance. I agree to knock of 10 percent. The customer grudgingly agrees, no doubt, with a sense satisfaction gained from haranguing me into submission."

Although popular writers harp on the advantage of cooperative negotiation, Professor Gerald Williams, in an article titled, "Style and Effectiveness in Negotiation," reports that aggressive negotiators can be effective.

Techniques that Work with Aggressive Negotiators

In all negotiations, it is essential to do your homework. Know the facts, figures and other data. An "I'll ask for more, no matter what the other person offers," is a bad strategy. To get a fair deal, you must be able to recognize one when you see one.

Two aggressors can likely reach an agreement. They understand attacking strategies and most are willing to give a bit to reach a settlement. However, they will take longer and use up more resources before they agree.

If your opponent negotiates aggressively, you will likely do better by also taking an aggressive stance. Understand there may be some unnecessary posturing and babbling. This is to be expected. Do not take it personal. In your offers, leave some room for compromises. Aggressors expect this.

Do not try to cooperate with an aggressor. Neither side will understand each other. Aggressors see cooperatives as naïve, opportunities to be plucked. Cooperatives get their feelings hurt and wish to avoid the sordid mess. Most stalled negotiations are of this mix.

Whatever the strategy, in the final analysis, both parties must see their outcome as fair. We delude ourselves when we think we can outwit car dealers, vendors, managers or employees. We simply are not smart enough, big enough or bad enough to consistently take advantage of other parties.

C. Effective Negotiators Use Reasonable Tactics

After your cousin calls you with the good news, "We bought the house," the next utterance is a predictable, "We got a really good deal!" At the same time the seller says to his relatives, "We sold our house. We got a good price."

Which party is delusional? Maybe both. Maybe neither.

In business dealings, research shows that less effective negotiators spend as much time planning their negotiations as the more effective negotiators. However, more effective negotiators differ in their tactics.

Just be Reasonable

Effective negotiators are reasonable. They understand that to continue to do business, the other party must get something out of the deal. After the deal, both sides should be better off. Negotiators, who insist on "winning" at the expense of other parties eventually find fewer people who will deal with them fairly.

Go into Negotiations with High and Low Ranges

Less effective negotiations go in with a fixed point. Or, they enter negotiations with no target such as, "I'm after the best deal I can get." More effective negotiators begin with upper and lower ranges on the bargaining factors. They base their ranges on research of market conditions.

Suggest Several Workable Options

Effective negotiators think in terms of options, alternatives, and multiple solutions. Several bargaining factors—price, delivery dates, quality, reliability, convenience, service—accompany even simple negotiations. Many combinations of these options may be satisfactory.

Be Cautious when Making Counter Proposals

In most negotiations, there comes a time for you to respond to the other's offer. Rather than a simple "accept" or "reject," you may consider a counter-proposal. If so, be deliberate. Less effective negotiators make counterproposals more quickly than do the more successful negotiators.

Focus on a Few Good Reasons

Negotiators understand how the deal will benefit them. Good ones also understand why the deal benefits the other party. There may be many potential benefits to the other party, but the more successful negotiators focus on just the major one or two reasons. If you litter your arguments with endless reasons "why," you are utilizing tactics of the less successful.

Do Not Over Sell Your Position

Less successful negotiators use words that may over sell or even over promise benefits, such as, "the best quality available," "you won't beat our price," "the most dependable," or "outstanding service." More successful negotiators purposefully avoid such phrases. They substitute more factual data such as actual quality measures, or prices compared to competitors, and the like.

Be Willing to Share Your Information

Successful negotiators appropriately share information. Begin with non-critical information, perhaps: inventory available, on time delivery record, lists of satisfied clients. As trust increases, negotiators may report even more critical information, including sales growth or decline, certain budget numbers, perhaps even cost structure.

Learn Something about the Other Party

Find out about the history, practices, partnerships, and philosophy of the other company.

Garner specific information about the individuals you are dealing with—work histories, areas of expertise, reputations. Seek personal information also—hobbies, school ties, family situations.

Negotiations go best when both sides understand and trust each other. Very few of us continuously get good deals for ourselves simply by out maneuvering the other party.

D. In Addition to Being the Right Thing to Do, Ethical Negotiation is Good for Business

Is it ethical for a person to roll back the miles on a used vehicle for sale? "Of course not."

Is it ethical for a prospective buyer to say to the seller, "I have an offer from someone else with a similar car that is almost a $1,000 less than what you are asking." All would agree that this would be ethical if it is accurate. But what if the offer is only $500 less?

Get ready for a debate. Some say that is close enough. The buyer said "almost." Others say, "Half of a $1,000 is not 'almost.'"

Attempts to Deceive in Negotiations are Unethical

Is it unethical to deliberately falsify documentation? Purposefully guarantee things you know you cannot deliver? Lie about a feature? Intentionally mislead the other party? Yes, yes, and yes.

But everything is not so black and white. What about the grey areas? You can get heated debates from well-meaning, upstanding citizens on whether the following are unethical:

- Making slight exaggerations.
- Refusing to reveal information that would help the other party.

• Avoiding answering questions that would weaken your position.
• Attacking the other party's data without justification.
• Pretending an offer is out of line when your data suggests it is not.
• Stating you will need your boss's approval when you do not.

What about this one? You need a report from a specialist in another department by a certain date, say November 16. Do you put a deadline of November 10 just to give yourself a little fudge room? Is that OK?

Guidelines for Ethical Negotiating Tactics

Set high standards for ethics in negotiations. Consider the following:

1. Is my statement or claim honest as I understand it? If you answer "No," to this question, I think it fails the ethics test point blank. Honesty is a minimum standard.
2. What about a grey area? Ask yourself, "Would I want the other person to use the tactic on me?" If the answer is, "No," then do not use the tactic on the other party. Most of us would certainly prefer doing business with persons that we trust to be straight shooters.
3. Consider the following guideline, "Will the tactic produce a good result for both parties?" Suppose a tactic produces a big "win" for you, but it comes at a big "loss" for the other party?

I suppose some are OK with getting a big "win" at the expense of a big "loss" for the other party. Even if you are comfortable with the ethics of this, ask the question, "Is it a good practice?"

Not only are high ethical negotiation standards the right thing to do, they are good for business.

Chapter 16: Influence

◆

(If you request and others respond, you have influence.)

If you request information from a coworker in another department and the coworker provides the information, you have influence. If you recommend that your boss cut down the time spent in meetings and the boss responds, you have influence. If you suggest that a staff member redo work to correct errors and the staff member complies, you have influence.

Influence is simply the ability to get others to comply with your requests and suggestions. Managers have legitimate authority because of their positions. Further, managers have rewards and sanctions that they can use to influence their subordinates.

However, many times we have a need to influence individuals even though we have no managerial position over them; that is, they do not report to us. And some individuals in managerial positions actually do not have much influence, even though they have the position and the title.

The ability to influence others is an art, but researchers have identified how influential persons get others to do things.

A. Five Proven Tactics for Increasing Your Influence

You have influence when your spouse responds to a request, when your children obey or when your dog sits on command. You really have influence if your cat comes when called.

You have influence when your employees listen to your advice, follow your suggestions, do what you ask them to do, or refrain from doing what you prohibit. You really have influence if you are able to cajole a stubborn person in another department to cooperate.

Influence is the essence of leadership. Most of us would like more influence. Our professional lives (not to mention our personal lives) would be much easier if we just had more influence.

Talk More

In a meeting, do most people talk more than you? If so, you could probably increase your influence simply by talking more.

"I had a real urge to say something," explained a shy person. "I was just not sure how others would take my suggestions." If you have ever had this feeling, you probably should talk more.

Express yourself. It is not necessary to always be right. Every idea need not be award winning. If you remain silent, your chances of influencing others just about equal the odds of winning the lottery, with or without a ticket.

Persist

If at first you do not succeed in swaying others to your way, try and try again. If you cave at the first sign of resistance, how can you earn the confidence of others?

Few good ideas are greeted with an immediate, "Sure, I'll do my part." If you believe something to be right, persist. Fight for your rights down to the last detail. Not with belligerence but with confidence. Show a little calm assurance as you face opposing forces.

Support Others

When a friend or foe offers good ideas, support him. Back him publicly. When others see you as an ally in their causes, you can more easily enlist their support in your campaigns. Be sincere. This is more than "Scratch my back and I'll scratch yours." If you politick just to get a favor, you are more likely to get backlash than cooperation.

Make Specific Requests

One of the reasons some people have influence is that they are crystal clear with their requests.

Never use ASAP (as soon as possible) in a request. Most interpret ASAP to mean, "When I can get around to it." Likewise, do not admonish anyone to "just do the best you can." And if it is correct for you to say "No" to a request, simply say, "No." Avoid vague responses such as "perhaps," "if certain conditions prevail," "I'll see," and "I'll get back to you."

I heard one manager say, "I'd like for you to make every effort to get the project completed in an efficient manner." In a similar circumstance, I heard another manager say, "I expect the project to be completed by the October 1 due date. Are we all clear on that?" Specifics improve your odds.

Confront Abusers

When someone lets you down, let him know about it. Express your displeasure, even your anger (no hitting, of course). People who take advantage do not have automatic sensors that correct their behaviors. Rather, abusive behavior not confronted tends to be repeated.

Influential people, like everyone else, do not like to be wronged. But unlike everyone else, influential people will call you out if you fail them. These suggestions may not always influence your teenager to go out of his way to pick up your clothes at the cleaners, but they will likely increase your odds.

B. Influence is More about What You Do than What You Say

When you scrape away all of the frills, a lot of your success depends upon your ability to influence others. A manager says to her staff, "We need to get this project completed on schedule. A very important customer is depending on us."

Staff members focus, adrenaline pumps, cooperation increases, and they get the job done. This manager exercised influence.

Another manager says to an employee, "You have used twelve days of sick leave and you have been late six times just within the past nine months. I really need for you to come to work more often."

The employee argues, makes excuses, blames the manager for lack of understanding and continues to miss work. This manager did not exercise influence.

Leaders are more influential when their words and actions match.

Some Dogs Don't Bark and Don't Bite

A manager said to me, "I have two employees who make too many mistakes. They do the bare minimum and they gripe a lot."

"What have you done?"

"They have been trained and they know their jobs. Other employees tell me they acted that way under the previous manager. I don't know what to do."

As sure as night follows day, if this manager says nothing and does nothing, the two employees will continue their current bad behaviors.

Some Dogs Bark but Don't Bite

Suppose the manager asks the whining, mistake-prone, low performers to be more attentive and offers coaching tips for reducing mistakes. The employees respond by arguing and blaming others.

The employees continue making mistakes. In the next encounter, the manager is less patient, "We've discussed this before, but you continue making careless mistakes. Now, you must be more careful!" Employees continue making mistakes and arguing.

Words without actions also register low on the influence scale. We soon learn which barking dogs are all bluff.

Some Dogs Bite without Barking

"You had better watch this one," an employee said in describing a new manager. "I knew him from a previous assignment. You never know where you stand. He'll stab you in the back in a heartbeat."

Managers who act without warning build resentment and distrust. They destroy employee commitment. Most people will do what they know they are supposed to do and that is all. These leaders stifle initiative and cooperative problem-solving. Like quiet, biting dogs, we fear them and try to avoid them at all costs.

Some Dogs Bark before They Bite

The best way to get most employees to do or not do something is to tell them in very clear terms what you want. Even gifted employees cannot read your mind.

If an employee makes too many mistakes, approach him with data. For example, "Harry, last week we got two complaints from customers about your work. You must serve our customers without upsetting them. You have been well-trained. If the complaints continue, you could be subject to our disciplinary process."

Should the employee continue performing poorly, the leader must record some disciplinary action, consistent with company policy, of course.

If a person says to a leader, "I knew that is what you were going to do," there is a good chance this leader has influence. Employees are more likely to follow leaders they can predict. We are better able to predict our leaders when they tell us clearly what they are going to do and follow up with actions.

C. Increase Your Influence by Improving Your Relationship

"I need help from someone in another department, but I can't seem to persuade him to get the information to me on time. And when I do get it, something is usually left out or poorly done."

"What do you do?"

"He gets it to me late. I have to stay late and do extra research so that I can meet my deadlines."

"Have you explained to the other person precisely what you need, when you need it, and why you need it?"

"Yes, several times. My efforts have not solved the problem."

How do others influence you when the other is not your boss

How do you influence people to do things for you when you have no authority over them? To answer this question, turn it around. How do people influence you when they are not in your chain of command?

Recall a time when the requests from other departments stacked up on your desk like leaves on your patio after a fall rain. Some requests take a few minutes to respond to; others take several hours. You cannot do all of them at the same time. The person making the request is not your boss. In fact, your boss may not even know about the requests or the extra work they require.

How do you decide which requests to respond to first? Which do you put off or not respond to at all? Do you rank them according to how important you think they are? Does it matter whether or not you even know the other person? Do you simply respond in the order that they came in? Do you respond first to the person who yells like a pack of trapped hyenas?

Relationships are more Important than Substance

Studies show that past histories are more important than substance when trying to influence people in other departments.

How would you prioritize the following examples?

A. I do not respect the person making the request and I am not sure of the value of the project.

B. I like the person a lot, but I'm not sure what the project contributes to our mission.

C. I have a good relationship with the person making the request and the project is very important.

D. I do not respect the person, but the project is important to our mission.

If you selected Example C as your first priority, you are in the majority. But what do you rank as your second priority? Most people rank Examples B and D pretty close for second place, but Example B usually gets a slightly higher ranking.

Most of us will respond to others outside our chain of command when we have a respectful relationship and we consider the request to be important. If we have no relationship with other parties, their influence is likely to be minimal. If our relationship has been as cantankerous as the feuding McCoys, we are likely to put so many other "important" items in front of the request; we may not be able to get to it.

The bottom line is, "To increase your influence, improve your relationship." Improve your relationship by getting to know the person, look for ways to help him, and try to understand his responsibilities better. A better relationship does not guarantee that you will always get the response you want. It does greatly improve your odds.

D. Consider Using "Currencies" to Influence Others

According to Webster "currency," which comes from the Latin word *currentia,* means "any form of money that is in actual use as a medium of exchange." In our economy, currency may refer to paper money, bank notes, bills, certificates, Federal Reserve notes, or greenbacks—as in a greenback dollar bill.

What are the Currencies of Influence?

Of course, people want money. And if leaders had boat loads of money, they could influence even slothful souls to exert some perspiration in service of the mission. But money alone is a very expensive way of influencing. And people will put their shoulders to the grindstone for non monetary, intangibles that we cannot see, taste or hold.

In the fuzzy language of influence, "*currencies*" refer to tangible and intangible things that are important to people, something they value, something they want.

Leaders know well that many of us value attention. Thus, we say that a staff member trades in the currency of attention when he exchanges his effort for a response from a boss such as, "Great job, Robert! I want all of you to take notice of the tremendous contribution that Robert has made to our team."

In their book, *Influence Without Authority,* authors Allan Cohen and David Bradford list five types of currencies available to most of us.

Some People Respond to the Currency of Inspiration

Some people do things because the activity is meaningful to their lives.

When explaining why she went to an extraordinary effort to serve a client, the employee said, "I did it because it was simply the right thing to do." People still do things because they are morally and ethically correct.

Exciting visions, meaningful missions, an opportunity to perform superbly or achieve excellence are other examples of inspiration-related currencies.

Anything that Helps another Person Complete Tasks is a Currency

Anything that helps get the task done represents a task-related currency. Extra budget, people, tools, equipment, and space are examples. Other examples include: additional responsibility, opportunity for a challenge, information, public support, assistance, quick responses and behind-the-scenes help.

Status Enhancements are Currencies

Position currencies are related to things that will help persons enhance their position and status in the organization. "Even though there was no extra pay, I took the assignment," explained an employee, "because I knew that the outcome would be highly visible to the owners. I would be well positioned for the future."

An opportunity to gain reputation, make contacts, and look good in front of the right people are also examples of position-related currencies.

Many People Value Relationships as Currencies

Many people desire and seek enriched, meaningful relationships. When you provide sincere personal support, sympathy, understanding or acceptance, you are supplying things that are of value to some people—thus these offerings can be influence currencies.

The Opportunity to have an Impact is a Currency

Personal currencies add to an individual's sense of self worth. Such currencies make us feel more complete. To have an impact, to make a contribution, to be more secure, and to reach a comfort level are examples of personal currencies.

Most of Us have Access to these Currencies

Yes, all of us have access to these kinds of currencies. And unlike money, we do not deplete our resources when we exchange these currencies for things that are important to us.

As with any tool, the concept of currencies—as in, "I will recognize you if you do what I want"—has the potential for misuse. Dishonest, deceitful, self-serving and unscrupulous individuals do attempt to manipulate others into doing things. But when the person attempting to influence is honest and has good motives, currencies become a useful, ethical tool for influencing others.

E. How to Influence Peers in Other Departments

"One of the most frustrating parts of my job," explained an office employee, "is getting information that I need from people in other departments in a timely fashion. One person in particular is always, and I mean always, late."

The employee explained that every two weeks she had to stay late on Tuesdays so that she could get her job completed by the Wednesday deadline.

"Have you clearly explained why you need it on time?" I asked.

"Yes, many times."

"Have you told the person that you have to stay late because he does not get his part of the analysis to you on time?"

"He knows."

"Have you asked him if there was any way that you could help to ensure that he finishes on time?"

"We've talked several times. He says he's just so busy. He promises to do better. And he might for a time or two. Then he's back to his old habits. He is just a procrastinator."

Almost 70 percent of office employees say that they frequently or occasionally get frustrated because they do not get timely cooperation from someone in another department.

Be Aware When the Other Party is Taking Advantage

The employee in the example above did exactly what she should have done. She explained the reasons for the deadline, let him know that his behavior caused her to work late and offered to help the procrastinating dolt.

This is a tough case. Many conscientious producers eventually give in and merely accept "doing extra work" like working late as part of the job. While it might work for the organization, it increases my bile to see high performing employees consistently support poor performers in other departments.

Such codependent behavior is unfair to high performers. And it rewards the poor performers by shielding them from the consequences of their behaviors.

How to Manage the Peer Who does not Cooperate

Consider this. For several weeks, keep specific notes on violations, for example, number of times late, dates, extra hours worked, number of reminding phone calls, dates of offers to help, and the like.

Show the information to your boss. Say something like, "I want to be a good team player. I am very willing to extend myself to help others. Given the long term repetitive experience with this person, I think my cooperative efforts are being abused."

Likely, the boss will understand, offer sympathy and perhaps intervene. Also, it is likely that the boss's intervention will help for a while. Soon though, the boss will necessarily have to divert her attention elsewhere and the procrastinator will resort to form.

At this point, the cooperative employee has an opportunity to get creative. Perhaps she can estimate (or guess) what the procrastinator should have provided and complete the report using estimates of the missing analysis.

Note clearly that you have merely filled in the blanks with a guess because the actual data did not arrive in time.

If this suggestion is impractical, you have one last resort. Say to the person, "I've continuously extended myself to cover for you. Beginning next week, do not expect me to continue. This is unfair to me and it encourages inefficiency on your part."

Let your boss know what you are doing. You may put yourself at some risk. Should you decide that it is not worth the risk, then accept your fate graciously. Translation, quit complaining. Focus on the things you like about your work.

F. How to Influence with Rational Appeals, Inspiration and Consultation

Most of us long for more influence, as in, "If I could just get my boss to (fill in the blank), my job would be so much easier." It is also frustrating when you have to depend on someone in another department who is about as responsive as a single-toed sloth.

Even if you are the boss, it does not mean that all of your staff members will cater to your requests as if you were Mary, Queen of Scots. Influence is the ability to get others to do things, hopefully willingly and with enthusiasm. How do you do this without the use of heavy artillery?

According to researcher G. R. Ferris, rational persuasion, inspirational appeals and consultation tend to be the most effective means of getting others to do or to refrain from doing things.

Many People Respond to Rational Appeals

A manager proposed to his boss, "We need to update ten workstations in my department."

The boss replied, "How much money will it save us?"

"Oh, it won't save us any money."

"Well, then how much revenue will it generate?"

"I don't think it will generate any additional revenue."

"Tell me again why I should invest the money to update the workstations."

"We would be able to do a lot more things than we are currently doing, and we would be more efficient."

This argument is vague and general. It is not persuasive. To persuade rationally, provide data, facts, tangible cost reductions, proof of added value, and other believable information. Give documented, logical arguments. Be specific.

I have yet to see a leader turn down a request that had a believable and significant benefit-to-cost ratio.

Consider Inspirational Appeals

Appeal to individuals to do things because they serve a worthy mission. Show how customers will benefit. Owners benefit. Employees are better off. It will improve humankind. Just doing the right thing is a significant persuader for many people.

I observed a manager, when requesting extraordinary effort from a repair crew, use an inspirational appeal. After making the request, the manager said, "For the next twenty-four hours, you have the most important assignment in the entire company."

The crew looked askance and smiled unbelievingly. "No, I mean it," he said. "We have an entire shipment held up in Houston. They can't leave until you complete this repair. Thousands of our customers are waiting on you." The crew immediately perked up and renewed their focus on the task at hand.

Of course, to be effective, the appeal must be honest. People see through BS like it was a clear plate glass window.

Sincerely Requesting Input often Encourages Cooperation

Rather than merely requesting or demanding something, check with others about their opinions. Make requests. Seek alternatives. Ask people what they think. Try out your idea on them. Present a thought and ask for improvements.

For instance, "I'm thinking about adding more analysis to the project, but I would need your part within a couple of weeks. Do you think the analysis would add value? Can I help you get your part done?" People are much more cooperative on endeavors they help design.

Again, be honest. Do not ask for others' suggestions unless you are willing to listen with an open mind.

Do not misunderstand. These appeals will not turn self-serving, spiteful, arrogant, uncooperative individuals into smiling team players. Further, the use of these tools does not guarantee that you always get your way, but they can, and often do, get results.

Chapter 17: Morale

◆

(To get high morale, you must first have good performance.)

All managers want good morale. In fact, almost sixty percent of the managers we survey say that morale is more important than performance. While I disagree with this statement, I do agree that morale is very important.

Morale, sometimes called job satisfaction, is the degree to which employees feel good about themselves and their work place. Employees with good morale tend to be upbeat and pleased with their work situation. A group with bad morale is usually frustrated, unhappy and may show little commitment to their companies.

I think we know how to create good morale in work groups, but I am often surprised when I see managers attempting superficial and short-term tactics for improving morale.

A. Hiring, Job Fit and Company Success Contribute to Morale

"The beatings will continue until morale improves!" is a saying that probably originated from some unknown wit trying to poke fun at his company's efforts to improve morale.

Sometimes it seems that the above statement, intended to be satire, may hold more truth than we think. In a meeting with a vice president and 65 employees, one employee blurted out, "What are you going to do about the low morale in our division?"

Without blinking an eye, the vice president responded, "I've visited several other divisions and the morale is just as low in other divisions as it is here."

I am not sure what the leader intended to communicate. I do know that most thought the implication of the VP's statement was, "Quit whining. You're better off than most."

I overheard another leader harshly comment, in response to a question about morale, "If we have a morale problem around here, I sure want to know about it!"

Given the frown on the leader's face, I doubt many employees believed him.

Three Proven Practices for Creating Good Morale

Good morale in the workplace generally means that employees feel good about coming to work. Their mood, state of mind and outlook are positive. People with good morale are satisfied with their jobs.

Typical efforts to create good morale center on company picnics, golf outings, bagels on Friday, employee recognition programs and the like. While I endorse these efforts, they are not sufficient to maintain good morale.

To create and sustain good employee morale, leaders must do the following.

1. **Hire happy people.** Studies show that genetics (not environment) explain a large percent of a person's happiness. Further, an individual who has positive feelings about one company (manager, location, profession) will still have positive feelings if their employment conditions change. Put differently, you cannot hire maladjusted, trouble-making, faultfinders and expect to create happy employees. What you hire is what you get.

2. **Create a good job fit.** Hire people who have the talents to do the job that you put them in. Select people who possess the ability and desire to do what you ask them to do.

   For detailed work, hire people who are good at detail. If customer satisfaction is important, hire empathic people. If employees are required to work in teams, hire people with cooperative personalities. People like to use their natural skills and abilities. A good job fit means that you have hired a person to do a job that she/he naturally does well.

   When employees have trouble learning and adapting to job requirements quickly, it is a pretty good indication that you do not have a good job fit. Rather than continue the struggle, it is better to change the job or move the person to another position. If neither is practical, do the employee and the company a favor and professionally let them go.

3. **Make the team successful.** People like success. If you are behind schedule and over budget; and if customers are unhappy and sales are falling faster than the Dow in a recession, you cannot expect people to have good morale.

During troubled times, leaders should do whatever is necessary (legally, ethically and morally, of course) to fix the situation. Solutions may mean extra work, overtime, and additional customer services, foregoing pay increases, even layoffs.

In the short run, such actions may pressure morale downward. But nothing dampens employee morale faster than company failures. The sooner you can return to success, the quicker morale will improve.

B. Do Not Let Misplaced Compassion Get in the Way of Improving Morale

Identify whether you think the following tend to be "true" or "false."

1. Low performance leads to low morale.
2. Employee morale is more important than performance.
3. An effective way to increase performance is to improve morale.
4. A strong display of compassion may unintentionally lower morale.
5. It is undesirable to have high morale when performance is low.
6. A major way to improve morale is to improve performance.
7. Many leaders worry too much about morale.

Although not everyone will agree, count the following answers as correct: 1 = true, 2 = false, 3 = false, 4 = true, 5 = true, 6 = true, 7 = true.

No matter how good you are at human relations, if you are leading an eighth place team in an eight-team league, morale will be lower than the prices of last year's high fashion shoes. If you were to have good morale on a last place team; now that would be a problem! We do not need happy people when we are losing.

Performance Precedes Morale

We like success. Employees wish to be successful in their jobs. People want to work for successful companies. We want our kids to be successful. It makes us happy when we do well. It is hard to have happy people, or happy leaders for that matter, when the department is over budget, under the goal and behind schedule.

A leader asked me if I could improve the morale of his group. I said I would try. In my first visit with the group, I asked, "Are you experiencing any performance problems?"

"Oh, yes," they replied. "We've just lost our biggest account and it looks like two others are about to go to our competitor. Volume is off 20 percent compared to last year."

"You seem to be pretty low," I said to the group.

"Yes, we are," they replied. "What can we do to improve our morale?"

"You will not like my answer," I said, "but if you want to improve your morale, you have to get your accounts back. If that means lowering prices, working on weekends, passing on pay increases, cutting your support budget, or working with less staff, that is what you do."

When you get your customers' business back, you can celebrate and award bonuses. Then and only then will morale be higher. We get good morale by celebrating high performance. We do not get high performance by striving for high morale.

Do Not Confuse Compassion with Morale

It seems paradoxical, but when morale is lowest, leaders may need to be more demanding and less compassionate.

A performance wreck requires true leadership. This is not the time to feel sorry for the group. Hand-wringing participation meetings are not helpful. Forget about demanding more resources from top management. What good does it do to wallow in the misery of failed expectations?

Leaders may have to ask people to do things they do not want to do like work extra hours, forego pay increases, attend additional training sessions, or change their work schedules. Too much compassion may simply add to the problem. "I don't want to ask them work on Saturday," said a leader, "They are unhappy enough already."

In reality, the group may need to work Saturday to keep from sliding into a darker hole.

When morale is low, leadership should first identify a plan for righting the ship and getting performance back on course. Do what it takes—legally and ethically—to be successful.

The shared celebration of exceeding expectations while coming in under budget is the best tonic for improving employee morale.

C. How to Maintain High Morale During Economic Downturns

How do you maintain employee morale when the economy goes south? The answer to this question may be as elusive as the fountain of youth. Check all of the following that you think have a significant impact on boosting morale while sales and profits are tanking:

1. Extra sensitivity to employees' personal situations.
2. Greater tolerance of employee mistakes.
3. Sponsorship of "fun events."
4. A realistic, tough plan to increase sales and profits.
5. Leader optimism.
6. Firm expectations of employee performance.

In my experience, only Numbers 4, 5, and 6 hold much hope of recapturing good morale.

Performance Must First Increase

Even people with "rose-colored glasses" do not associate high morale with declining sales and profits. Companies who are on the fast track to bankruptcy have no right to expect good morale.

Make sure that you get a plan. Employees want to see a way out of the pain, and they look to leadership to provide a path.

When the economy wrecks, take whatever actions are needed (legally, ethically and morally) to turnaround performance. Cut prices, forego pay increases, increase delivery time, tighten employee policies, freeze spending, extend guarantees, pare all frills.

Do what it takes to get the customers back. Only when customers return and sales and profits increase can you realistically expect to achieve high employee morale.

Avoid Playing the Victim

No one may know for sure why the wreck happened, but it does little good to assume the role of victim and blame upper management, competitors, other nations, politicians, and predecessors. It is especially important for first-line managers and employees to avoid blaming the home office.

When leadership refocuses the organization's efforts, it usually causes inconveniences to all—no pay increases, increased demands, longer hours, even layoffs.

"They don't understand what we're going through," people lament. "All they are interested in is the bottom line."

Well, leadership should be focused on the bottom line! If there is no bottom line, there are no jobs. The company vanishes quicker than last season's fashions. Get on board with the top leader's plans. Managers and employees fare better when they support leadership's plan to improve.

Show Some Confidence in Your Leadership

Downturns are frightening. They can shake the very foundation of employees' dreams.

It does not help when leaders wring their hands and explain, "There is little we can do about it. Competition is up; the economy is in a slump; the future is uncertain; we're confused just like you are." Successful leaders believe. They believe in themselves and they believe in their ideas.

Show some confidence in the actions that you plan to take. I understand your vision into the future is not crystal clear. Keep researching and digging for ideas until you are confident that your plan has a good chance of succeeding. Then in the face of danger, execute the plan.

Avoid Over Identification with the Plight of Employees

Leaders who go to great efforts to support and protect their employees at all costs usually wind up with two unwanted outcomes.

One, many employees suffer more than necessary because leaders do not make the tough decisions necessary to survive and succeed. Two, they increase employee pain and drive morale even lower because the company continues to fail. The first, and most basic, requirement of good morale is company success!

D. What to Do When Your Morale is Low

"I'll tell you, I'm really not happy with the new software package," explained a high-performing employee. "It's not doing some of the things we wanted and vendor support is poor."

"What are you going to do about it?" I asked.

"I don't know. It's just frustrating. Sometimes I think it might be time for me to start looking for other opportunities."

From time to time, most of us are dissatisfied with something that is going on at work. To use a trite phrase, "That's just life." It is not so important that we are dissatisfied. How do we handle the frustration? That is the issue. Suppose your dissatisfaction meter is knocking past eight or nine? How do you deal with this?

Take Initiative and Try to Make the Situation Better

When dissatisfied, first offer suggestions for improvement. An executive once described his pet peeve as employees coming to him several weeks after a decision and accurately pointing out serious flaws in the decision.

The executive said, "As slow as I am, I understand now that we have some problems. I don't need people pointing that out. What I need are suggestions for how to fix them!"

Take the initiative. Change things that you can. Offer suggestions to others. Explore different alternatives for making it work. Be bold. Take some chances.

Consider Suffering in Silence

Suppose upper management refuses your brilliant suggestions or worse yet, ignores them. Now, what to do?

Consider shutting up. You have tried. For whatever reasons, you did not prevail. Can you still remain loyal? After all, the pay is probably good. You have some friends at work. You enjoy most of what you are doing. You get vacation time and a benefit package. You have a mortgage, youngsters in school.

You are having a little heartburn, but you can stay focused on your work. Companies and decisions go in cycles. Wait for things to improve, but do not keep flailing away at brick walls that you cannot move.

You may not be joyful, but at some point you have to accept the fact that your suggestions are not going to prevail. Maybe upper management knows something you do not. Above all, continue producing good work.

See if You Can Get Past the Issue

If your level of dissatisfaction is low, say a two or a three on a ten-point scale, just ignore it. Not everything is going to work your way. There are many ways of achieving good results. It may be that you are just upset that upper management did not choose your way.

Save your efforts for more meaningful issues. Keep your powder dry. Do not go into a funk and miss work. Get up. Get to work on time. Do your job well. It's probably OK to whine a little to a close friend, but do not let it get out of hand.

At Some Point, the Solution May Be to Leave

Suppose you have tried the above options and you still awaken at two a.m. in a cold sweat. Your stomach feels like it has a permanent knot in it. Your level of dissatisfaction is so high you cannot concentrate on your work. This has gone on for several months.

Perhaps you are not cut out for this organization. It may be time to pack your bags. Pay and benefits may not be worth the cost to your health.

It is physically and mentally unhealthy to stay on in a job when you are very, very dissatisfied for lengthy periods. Look for another job. Can you retire? Or maybe it's time to get serious about your long-held idea of starting your own business.

E. A Good Way to Become Unpopular is to Strive for Popularity

"Robinson was very supportive of his staff." "He would sure do you a favor if he could." "I think he wanted to make all of us happy." "He couldn't stand for anyone to be mad at him." "I think he was just too nice a person." "Everybody liked him."

Would you like to work for a manager like Robinson? Sounds like he would be a great boss—"very supportive," "doing people favors," "a nice person."

There was only one problem. During the two years that Robinson served as manager, performance and morale tanked. Things went all right, not great, the first few months. But a strong competitor moved into Robinson's territory. The competitor pressured Robinson's group with lower prices and more services.

When Robinson's numbers began sliding, the vice president suggested that Robinson look at his processes. Perhaps there were ways to increase efficiency or reduce costs. Robinson responded, "There is nothing wrong down here. The problem is in the home office where you treat people like a bunch of numbers!"

Home office personnel liked Robinson. He had been an excellent performer. As one executive said, "I don't know why Robinson can't get the job done. He has all of the tools. He has experience, a good record. I don't know where to fault him."

Another executive agreed but added, "He is a first-class person. But he is identifying more with his people than with the mission. He's putting so much pressure on himself; he is going to bust wide open. And you are not going to change him either."

Robinson made the classic mistake of trying to get people to like him. And he did succeed in being popular with his staff. Many people were also loyal and banded together with Robinson to criticize company leadership.

Below are a few symptoms of managers who put popularity ahead of performance.

"Popular" Leaders Advocate Strongly for Staff

"Popular" managers are quick to advocate for their people. At the first sign of trouble, they argue for more support, more budget, more staff, or all of the above. "Popular" managers may also seek relief by demanding more time or rationalizing why their performance goals were set too high in the first place.

When top executives continue requiring performance, "popular" managers criticize the home office, or owners, as the culprit for their troubles, sometimes using such phrases as, "They are just a bunch of investors. They are not interested in what we do."

Sometimes things get nasty. Managers may withhold information that makes them look bad. In extreme cases, "popular" managers may even color data to put themselves in a better light.

"Popular" Leaders are Quick with Excuses

"Popular" managers are very empathetic with their employees. They are quick to praise. They are very patient with employees' personal struggles. Such managers go to great lengths to prevent any blame from landing on the shoulders of their people. Excuses pop up like daisies in the spring. If an excuse is hard to find, popular managers blame bad luck.

"It was just our bad luck." "Our timing was bad." "Who could have guessed that they would do that?" "They (the competition) are going to use up their people."

"Popular" Leaders are Lax in Enforcing Policies

"Popular" managers are quick to make exceptions to policies, especially to policies that their people criticize.

"I don't think they (the home office) really understand what impact this policy has on us." Some managers even say to their staff, "I'm not going to enforce this policy until they make me do it."

Of course, many successful leaders are popular. Employees really like them. But most of these leaders did not set out to become popular. Their goal was to get performance and to be successful. Truly popular leaders give credit and rewards generously to their team after they achieve success. Popularity becomes a nice side effect of success.

Chapter 18: Attitudes

✦

(To improve attitudes, you must hire employees with good attitudes.)

Attitudes are composed of beliefs, feelings and action tendencies. All of us hold attitudes toward many things, including our work, companies and managers. We want employees with good attitudes. Positive attitudes make for a better work environment. Employees with good attitudes make work more enjoyable.

I believe that too many managers give too little consideration to attitude when hiring. As a result, employees with bad attitudes get into the work place. Rather than terminating bad attitudes, managers spend a lot of effort trying to turn them into more positive people. Seldom does this work. It is more effective to understand the nature of attitudes and deal with them in a more practical way.

A. Separate Myths from Facts when Dealing with Employee Attitudes

How do you handle employees who argue a lot? Complain about everything? Keep other employees in a dither? Act like know-it-alls? Boss other employees? Have bad attitudes? Are whiners?

These are frequently asked questions in management development workshops. All of the questions refer to the same type of abrasive employees. Abrasive behaviors are rooted in people's personalities and most cranky employee behavior is pretty predictable.

Below are myths and facts about abrasive employees.

Myth: Whining employees will be more cooperative with a new boss.

Fact: Employees who complain about the current boss will also complain about a new boss. They likely complained about the previous boss, as well.

No matter how different the style of a new leader, abrasive employees can see problems in every program. As one person put it, "Bosses may come and go, but whiners are as predictable as the robins in the spring."

Myth: A transfer is often a good option for complainers.

Fact: Transfers do not change employee personalities. The first few weeks in a new department may produce a cooperative spirit. But after a brief period, the flawed personality traits of a grump find their way to the surface.

Myth: Whiners behave differently when they get positions of responsibility.

Fact: It is a great mystery to me why complainers, when promoted, often engage in the same behaviors that they railed against when they were employees.

An employee constantly complained about, "…too much politics in this department." After receiving a position of greater responsibility, her first task was to gather her cronies to plot a strategy for staying in power.

Another employee proclaimed, "…management is too secretive." One of his first moves after being promoted was to develop a "secret" strategic plan.

Myth: Change what the complainer is complaining about and he or she will quit complaining.

Fact: When managers first encounter a complainer, they typically try to solve the problem.

"My employee complained about his weekend work schedule," commented a manager. "With great effort, I got it changed. Did I get a 'thank you' from the employee? No, he immediately began complaining about his computer and telephone equipment."

Even if you gave complainers everything they asked for, they would still complain. Why? Because complaining is a part of their personality. It has very little to do with the work or the boss.

Myth: By explaining the impact of disruptive behavior to employees, managers can stop bad attitudes from influencing others.

Fact: Too many managers exhibit an eternal hope, an unfounded optimism, that rational explanations will produce rational results. More typically, the more explanations negative employees receive, the more points they have to disagree with.

Myth: The company did something to cause employees to have bad attitudes.

Fact: Evidence suggests that most whiners displayed their losing attitudes long before they joined their present organization.

Put differently, few companies create employees with bad attitudes. Many companies, though, hire employees with bad attitudes.

Who knows for sure why some employees engage in disruptive, dysfunctional behaviors? It could be bad childhood experiences or bad genes; maybe they were potty trained too early.

B. Use Compassionate Discipline with an Argumentative, Whining Employee

"I'm very frustrated," explained a supervisor. "I've got an employee who is hard to get along with. He argues a lot. He tries to tell others how to do their jobs. He complains about everything. He refuses to do certain things."

"Is the employee a good worker?" I asked.

"Oh, yes. He's very good. Fast, accurate. He does miss more work than I'd like for him to."

"Do others complain about the employee?"

"Yes, they complain about him a lot. I think one person has actually quit because of him."

"How long has the employee behaved this way?"

"For as long as I've been here. More than a year."

"Have you talked to him about his behavior?"

"Yes, a couple of times. He just got mad. Put the blame on somebody else."

"Why don't you terminate the employee?"

"Well, I hate to. He's got small children. Jobs are hard to get. I know he needs the money."

The job of a supervisor is a tough one. Employees like the one described above can really dampen job satisfaction.

Employees with Attitudes are Not Likely to Change

I think a supervisor has to accept at least three realities about disruptive employees.

One, the employee has been that way a long time, and a supervisor, no matter how well meaning, is not going to change him.

Two, supervisors do not make good psychologists, therapists, social workers or mommies. Curing the employee's fractious behavior is neither your role nor your responsibility. Often, when you try to help, like explaining and giving numerous additional chances, you actually make the situation worse.

Three, the employee is not as fragile as you think. He's gotten by with this behavior for a long period and he has learned how to acquire sufficient food, clothing and shelter.

How to Use Compassionate Discipline

I recommend a compassionate disciplinary approach. Without anger, malice, or misplaced sympathy, simply tell the employee that such behaviors are not acceptable. Let him know if he continues to be disruptive, there could be consequences, even termination. Then ask the employee if there is anything that you can do to help him.

If you have an Employee Assistance Program (EAP), strongly recommend that he talk to your local EAP representative.

If the behavior continues, proceed through the disciplinary actions of your particular company. These likely will consist of documented warnings and written notices prior to a termination notice. Make sure that your human resources people and your boss are fully involved.

Remember, it is not the people you terminate that make your work life miserable. Rather, it is the people you should have terminated but did not.

C. If You are Not Going to Terminate Employees with Nuisance Attitudes, Learn to Tolerate Them

Patrick has a reputation of a whiner.

"He complains a lot," explained a co-worker. "It doesn't much matter what management puts forward, Patrick can find something wrong with it."

For example, management upgraded a software program. They wanted better cost data on projects. Prior to the change, management solicited input from all users. Many people made suggestions. Management listened. Almost immediately after installation of the software, to the surprise of no one, Patrick began expressing some "concerns."

"I don't know why we have to document everything," Patrick opined. "I spend more time documenting than doing the work. I'm not going to worry about it too much. They'll change it again anyway."

Patrick has been in the department for six years. His performance evaluations are "acceptable." Patrick's manager describes him as a nuisance.

"He'll eventually do most of what I ask him to do," she says. "He just has to complain for awhile."

Peers say Patrick is not a bad person, but he does get on their nerves sometimes. What to do about an employee like Patrick?

Learn How to Tolerate Nuisance Whiners

There are several options for dealing with the Patricks of the world.

About 25 percent of managers, who attend my workshops, recommend termination for Patrick. But termination would be difficult. He has accrued six years of acceptable performance evaluations. Plus, it is hard to get the documentation needed for termination on nuisance whining.

About 55 percent of managers say they would coach and counsel Patrick concerning his whining. Some say they would send him to programs on how to gain a positive attitude. One manager said, "I'd point out to Patrick that his whining is a problem. I'd ask him why he complained so much. And I'd try to mentor him into being more positive."

Sounds good, but this approach, in most cases, does not work. Whining is part of Patrick's personality and we do not change our personalities much, if at all.

I overheard a manager counseling a whiner after the CEO had met with the group. Of course, the irritating employee, during the question and answer session, offered several complaints.

After the session, the manager asked the employee, "Why do you always find something to complain about?"

"I've always been a complainer," said the employee. "My parents taught me to be skeptical. I guess it's in my genes."

About 20 percent of managers say they would stress Patrick's positive points. His overall performance is acceptable and he eventually does most of what you ask him to do. Some of his complaints are probably justified.

This approach probably will not do much to reduce Patrick's whining. It might create some resentment from peers who get raw nerves from having to listen to him.

Here is my view. Realistically, you are not going to terminate Patrick and you are not going to change him. You can make matters worse by making an issue out of it.

Score Patrick low on cooperation and attitude on his performance evaluations; otherwise basically ignore his behaviors. When peers complain about Patrick's gripping. Say to them, "If it bothers you, why don't you talk with him and ask him to stop."

When the peer refuses to do this and suggests that it is the manager's job to get Patrick straightened out, with a smile say to the employee, "Patrick is not bothering me."

D. Why Training Cannot Cure Attitude Problems

An acquaintance said to me, "I'd like to send a person to one of your workshops."

"I appreciate your support," I responded. "Do you have any particular expectations of what you want the workshop to achieve?"

"Yes, I do. The person has great technical skills, but he has no people skills. He is a real attitude problem."

"Give me an example."

"Last month, he got upset with a group of people in other departments. He thought they were not getting reports to him quickly enough. He sent seven people a terse email on a Friday afternoon requiring that they show up in his office for a meeting at 7:30 the next morning—Saturday."

The manager further explained that the employee had no formal authority to require such a meeting, and he had not talked with his boss or anyone else about the matter. The manager also added that the employee frequently argued with management and complained constantly.

I politely told my acquaintance, "I would welcome the person to the program, but I do not think I can cure the employee's attitude problems. You might want to consider several years of therapy as an alternative."

"I don't want to invest that much into the project," he said.

Employee Problems that Training Cannot Cure

Training programs cannot cure rude, insensitive and irritating behaviors. As the old saying goes, "You can't make a silk purse out of a sow's ear."

Some people are unaware of the impact they have on others. Their antennas do not interpret cues that show irritation, hurt, anger, and bewilderment. Such people have low social intelligence.

Affected individuals send strong verbal or nonverbal signals that erupt like volcanoes to the senses of most people. The person with low social intelligence does not register a ripple.

Further, training does not turn slow workers into fast workers. It does not create record-setting performers out of mistake-prone employees. Training does not cure attendance failures or persistent whiners.

I do not say training has no impact in these areas. Exposure to intense and lengthy training could show some noticeable improvements. But the improvements are likely to be slight and probably temporary.

Training Programs Can Help Make Good Performers Better

Training programs are excellent at making good people better. If a person has a good attitude and good social skills, training can make them even better. People who work fast or accurately will work even faster and more accurately with additional training.

Individuals who have a natural talent for a task will improve dramatically with training.

Take the example of teams. Organizations like to form people into teams. Many even offer excellent training in how to work in teams.

If individuals on a team are naturally inclined to work together, team training can have excellent results. But some contrary independents are just not comfortable in the "giving and taking" required of good teams. No amount of training will likely turn a group of malcontents into a smooth, functioning unit.

In short, you get the greatest returns by investing training time and expenditure in people who are already doing a pretty good job. People who naturally and quickly pick up skills take to training like a duck to water.

Intuitively, it may seem that training would benefit weak or problematic performers. They just have so much more room to improve, it seems. But we need to accept reality. The upside of a good performer is actually greater than the upside of a poor performer.

Chapter 19: Discipline

✦

(Every good leader has good discipline.)

The best way to create a disciplined organization is to hire disciplined people. And in my experience, the vast majority of managers do hire employees who want to do the right things. Most employees want to be productive, they want to get along, they want to serve customers, and they want to follow company policies. They even want their bosses to like them.

A small percentage of employees—5 percent, maybe even 10 percent in some organizations—require discipline. We are not sure how these people get in the organization. Perhaps they slipped through the cracks during the hiring or perhaps they were there when the current manager assumed leadership of the group.

Even though the number of problem-employees is small, they take up an inordinate amount of leaders' time. This does not have to be the case, and it should not be. It is better for all when leaders administer discipline promptly, fairly and effectively.

A. Stress Mission Over Discipline

I believe that every good leader has good discipline. I also believe that the more effective leaders approach discipline quite differently than less effective leaders.

Compare these two approaches.

This Leader Preaches Strong Discipline

"I believe in strong discipline," a leader explained to me. "We have policies and I enforce them. I expect all of my staff to work together for the good of the organization."

"Do you have much trouble with discipline?" I asked.

"Not really. I told my staff from day one that I expected them to comply with all of our policies all of the time. I inherited a couple of employees who had a habit of coming in late and missing too much work. I counseled with them extensively, warned them verbally several times, and even put written reprimands in their folders. One eventually quit. The other one started coming to work."

The manager also said that he had a couple of people whose performance was marginal. "I've spent a lot of time with them," he said. "They've got to learn that I will not accept marginal performance."

I talked to the employees who worked for this leader. They described him as firm but fair. Employees said the leader frequently reminded them of the need to follow policies. He often brought data to their meetings showing violations within the company. "He compliments our department for our good compliance record," explained an employee.

One employee remarked, "He relies too much on the company manual." Another said, "Our meetings are pretty sterile. We are trying to save time by streamlining some of our processes. We are not making much headway." Still another added, "People who follow the rules get along fine with our boss."

This Leader Sells Company Mission

"Our mission is to deliver safe, reliable and low-cost service to our customers," explained a leader. "I frequently remind my staff how important this is. We also have quarterly objectives that I expect my team to meet. I mention the status of these at every department meeting."

"Do you have any trouble with discipline?" I asked.

"I don't think so. I had a couple of employees who missed too much work. In about two sentences, I told them that our team needed them to be there. One responded well. I terminated the other one for excessive absenteeism. I didn't spend much time on it and I didn't make a big deal about it."

As an employee described this leader, "He is very supportive. He wants to hear your ideas. He'll tell you if he disagrees, but he'll give you a chance."

When I asked the employees if there were any disciplinary problems in the group, I got responses like: "No, he terminated an employee for excessive absenteeism, but the employee had it coming. We never really talk about discipline. But he makes darn sure we are always on track with our departmental objectives."

Prioritize Mission Over Discipline

Both of these leaders maintained good discipline. But employees clearly saw the first leader as a disciplinarian.

The second leader created a more supportive atmosphere, and at the same time, appropriately and quickly disciplined employees who needed it.

Leaders have a limited amount of time and energy. I believe the more effective leaders expend their energies on mission, objectives, and achievements. They have good discipline, but they manage it with low expenditures of time and energy.

B. Patience is Not a Virtue When Dealing with Problem Employees

"Do you think that some managers are too patient with employees who are not suited for the job?" a new, front-line manager asked.

"I don't *think* that some managers are too patient," I responded. "I *know* that some are too patient."

Regardless of the popularity of Donald Trump's television show, few managers like to utter the words, "You are fired!"

"I just kept hoping that I could get him to change," explained a manager who let a problem linger for years. Patience in dealing with problem employees is not a virtue. In fact, patience usually results in at least two bad things.

One, it is not fair to the other employees who have to work harder because a member of their team is not performing. Two, a nonperforming employee has little chance of fulfillment and job satisfaction.

Terminations Do Not Have to Be Career Enders

Joseph, a nice, likeable young man was usually late on assignments. He often got distracted and did not even complete some tasks. After he was terminated, he moved to another state and took a different job. A year later he called his former boss and cheerfully said, "I just wanted to let you know. I'm working with a company in Arizona and I'm doing really well."

While you may not produce this result each time you terminate an employee, you at least give the employee a chance to find a better fit.

Be Professional When Terminating Problem Employees

"I just can't help but feel badly for the guy," explained a manager. "He has a mortgage. I know he needs the money. If he would only apply himself, he could do it."

There are a lot of "if onlys" associated with keeping marginal employees. The truth is most sub-par employees are actually not capable of performing what is required. In reality, you have a misfit between the employee's talents and the job requirements.

I have studied numerous terminations and have been personally involved in more than a dozen. In one case, the board of a large company terminated its president. The entire series of discussions were polite and civil. It is quite possible to process terminations without acrimony.

In some cases, the parties even maintain a friendly relationship.

Visit with the employee at the first sign of a problem. If the employee has been absent, tell her you are concerned and explain your policy. If a worker makes a mistake, show him how to do it correctly. Tell slow workers that you expect them to complete the tasks by a specific time. Tell whiners to think more about the benefits of working there.

Ask employees with abrasive attitudes to stop it. Show them what team-work means to you.

After each "correction," encourage. Try something like, "Mary, I really need for you to be here. You have an important contribution to make. We're counting on you."

If, after a couple of corrections you see little or no improvement, give the employee a verbal warning. Talk with your Human Resources Manager to ensure that you follow your policy. Again, encourage the employee to improve. Try to find ways to support him.

If there is little or no improvement after a couple of verbal counseling's, lay out a specific improvement plan with dates and measurements. Encourage the employee again.

At this point, many employees will understand that they do not have a future in the job, and they will quit. Some will not. Proceed with termination. It is the best for the company and the employee.

C. Four Problem Employees and How to Handle Them

Fortunately for managers, most employees come to work on time, do their jobs and get along. But all managers have a few ingrates who do not want to get with the program.

In a broad sense, there are three ways to deal with problem employees: coach them to improvement; tolerate them the way they are (just put up with them); or terminate them. Employees who pose problems present their issues in one of four ways.

The Older but Nonproductive Employee

This problem person, usually fifty-five years of age or older, may have been with the company for several years. More managers than you can count have coached, counseled, cajoled, threatened and even begged the employee to do better.

But as one manager said, "He's gotten by with it for years. Why does he think we are going to do anything about it?"

Recommendation: Work with your Human Resources (HR) Department and set up a Personal Improvement Plan (PIP) for coaching the employee to improved performance. Build sanctions, including termination, into the plan. If the employee does not respond, apply the sanctions.

Caution: If you are not willing to terminate the employee, prepare to tolerate him. Your odds of getting lasting improvement are far less than your chances of hitting an inside straight on the river in a Texas Hold'em poker game. Let's face it. Most companies are not going to fire this employee. Save yourself a lot of trouble. Quit worrying about this person.

The Younger, Nonproductive Employee

This employee usually looked good in the interview, three weeks on the job he turns into a grouch and he makes mistakes. When approached, he always finds a way to blame others. Training does not help. Do not think that you can tighten the loose screws in his head and change him into the person he appeared to be during the interviews.

Recommendation: This is an easy one. Recognize that you made a mistake in hiring. Work with your Human Resources Department to terminate the employee now. If you overlook this problem employee, you are asking for trouble in the future.

The Productive Employee with a Bad Attitude

You should try coaching the employee once or twice on how to be more appreciative, cooperative, or friendly, but get real; you cannot change attitudes, so coaching will not likely work.

Recommendation: Tolerate the employee's whining and complaining. Do not continue coaching. Do not lecture. Listen emphatically to his irrational complaints and then ignore him.

Caution: If other employees quit because they cannot work with this person, you have to terminate him. No single employee is so good that you cannot function without him.

The Cooperative but Nonproductive Employee

"I would describe her as a sweet, young lady," explained the employee's supervisor.

"Then what's the problem?" I asked.

"She just doesn't seem to get it. She'll agree to any assignment, but unless I check on her several times a day, she will not complete the job. She visits too much and gets distracted. She'll even volunteer to help someone else when she hasn't completed her work. "

Recommendation: Terminate the nice, young lady. Attempts at coaching will only frustrate you. Release her now, before it is too late, and encourage her to find a job in a position that is more suitable to her tendencies.

Caution: Do not overlook performance deficiencies just because someone is a nice person. Your company invests a lot of assets in all employees. If you tolerate nonperformance, you jeopardize the jobs of others.

In summary, when dealing with problem employees, first try to coach them. If you do not get quick results, consider tolerating them. If their behavior is too disruptive, your only other option is termination.

D. Do Not Wait for a Down Cycle to Remove Bad Performers

When discussing the future of a very marginal performer, a manager commented, "The employee can get by with shoddy performance now."

"Why?" I asked.

"The economy is good. We're making money. It's hard to find good replacements. When the economy goes south, he'll be one of the layoffs."

I understand that some managers use economic downturns to flush marginal employees from the system. I think this practice is delusional and unfair.

Keeping Bad Performers During Growth Sacrifices Upside

Think what you are doing when you purposefully keep nonproducers on the payroll. You are sacrificing upside potential because you are getting a poor return on your investment. If you replaced the nonperformers with better ones, your company would be even more successful.

Further, I think companies take advantage of their better employees when they keep laggards on the payroll. As a good producer said, "We would have higher customer satisfaction if we got rid of a couple of bad attitude employees."

In an internal survey, one company asked employees what they could do to improve product quality. Several employees wrote in suggestions like, "Get rid of the deadwood." Good employees lose opportunities for additional earnings and promotions when they have to drag less motivated nonperformers along.

Avoid Creating a Culture of Accepting Marginal Performances

"I've got an employee who is not doing his job," commented a manager, "but in our culture it is very hard to fire anyone."

Few managers really want to fire employees. Many managers harbor guilt feelings about terminations. They believe that it is somehow their fault. One manager commented, "I feel sorry for the poor guy. I don't know what he would do if he didn't have this job. He's probably not qualified for the job and he misses too much work. Anyway, our company has a history of not terminating people."

A company culture of protecting unacceptable performances gives hesitant managers a rationale for 'living with' the consequences of poor performance.

It is Unfair to Marginal Performers

I think it is even unfair to nonperformers to carry them along when the company is prospering. To survive, companies may have to let them go when profits sour. The up cycle may last for several years. During this time employees adjust their standard of living to their salary and benefits, and they get a year older each year.

It is far better to release people during the good times. Because the economy is booming, they have better chances of getting on with other companies—hopefully, in a job that better suits their particular talents. If they can do this when they are younger, adjustments are much easier to make.

Do Not Use the Crutch of "It's Hard to Find Replacements"

"If we were to let her go, a replacement would likely be just as bad, maybe even worse," a manager explained. I think this is just an excuse to avoid making termination decisions.

Sure, it is hard to hire good people during good times. But the hiring challenge is the same during both good and bad times. Whether the labor supply is scarce or plentiful, your challenge is to hire better talent than your competitors.

When you have many applicants for a job, your competitors also have many choices. It's a false security to assume hiring is easier during slow periods. No matter how qualified a hire may be, if your competitors are recruiting more talented employees, they will still beat you in the marketplace.

No matter how you slice it, your long-term success requires that you recruit and retain more talented employees than your competition.

E. "Terminate" is Not Always a Bad Word

The line, "You're fired!" may have been popularized on television shows, but most managers, in real life, would rather be caught in a cheap suit than use the word "fired," or "terminated," or "dismissed."

Even when the economy is going downhill faster than a spring avalanche, managers do not "lay off" people. They "right size."

Although the words scare us, the concept terrifies us more. Too many managers, emboldened by human resources specialists, do not consider termination as an option.

How do many managers handle blatant policy violators or anemic performers? They just try to keep pulling a rabbit out of a hat, thinking that surely there must be some way to get their attention.

I have asked hundreds of managers, "Have you ever, in your career, recommended termination of an employee?"

Only about 45 percent respond, "Yes."

Of the 45 percent, I ask, "After you have had time to reflect upon your termination recommendation, do you believe it was the right decision?" One hundred percent say, "Yes." In fact, most are extremely confident that they made the right decision. Many say, "The only problem is that I waited much too long to do it."

A Termination often Improves both Situations

I believe that proper terminations often improve both the company and employee's situation.

Matt, an outgoing, well-liked young professional, was great meeting with people. He was horrible at following through. He convincingly promised proposals and responses. His execution consisted of mistakes and apologies for missed deadlines. Although disappointed at being let go, Matt flourished in his next job.

Although Donald promised to complete his licensing credentials by a date certain, he did not. His manager said, "Donald, I have no choice but to let you go." Although Donald had a passel of excuses for being late, the boss did not accept them. Donald had a great career in another industry.

When she first took the job, April performed well. However, new regulations and increased work volume required more than April could handle. A skyrocketing stress level accompanied her performance decline. After she was terminated, she earned more money with another company. "I am much, much happier," she added.

Abraham Lincoln, former President of the United States, was fired. So was Lee Iacocca, former president of The Chrysler Corporation. Both had great success after hearing the words, "You're fired."

Few people are happy when their work lives fail. They know they are not doing a good job. Their friends know it. Their families know it. One person said the actual termination was surprisingly a relief. "I just felt like a deadman walking," he said.

Another said, "I should have quit myself, but I just did not have the courage. I was afraid to quit. When the boss gave me the dreaded release, I took the painful steps of finding another job. I think I got it right this time."

Allow the Employee to Depart with Dignity

Termination should never be a surprise. Give the employee two or three chances to improve. Show data on unacceptable performances. Offer suggestions for improvement. Identify time tables and deadlines.

Try to leave a little dignity on the table. Let the employee know that you feel badly that it did not work. Explain that it just was not a correct fit. Be supportive in helping with another career in another company.

F. You Can Terminate Employees for Their Off-the-Job Behavior

"My company does not control my life. What I do on my own time is my personal business," is the way a new employee expressed her feelings about some of her company's policies.

This raises the issue: "Just how much control does (or should) companies have over the off-duty behavior of their employees?"

Which, if any, of the following could be cause for dismissal at your organization?

- Arrest and conviction for drug use
- Personal use of company vehicle
- Public conduct that directly damages the company image
- Marital affairs
- Conviction for shoplifting

As author, Carolyn Hirschman reports in her article, "Off Duty, Out of Work," appearing in the February, 2003 issue of *HR Magazine,* the answers to these issues may not be crystal clear.

Guidelines for Off-the-Job Conduct

Although state laws vary, some off-duty conduct is legally protected. Some is not. Other activities fall into a murky area.

Legally Protected Conduct. Many states operate under an "employment at will" concept, meaning employees can be terminated for any reason that is not illegal. However, the federal government protects employees against terminations based on such things as religion, sex, age, disability, pregnancy, or whistle blowing.

Conduct that May Not Be Protected. In a recent case, a male, married employee liked to dress as a woman. He used make-up, wore women's shoes, dresses and, yes, women's undergarments.

Because the cross dresser frequently flaunted his dress in public, management terminated the employee on the basis that this behavior was bad for their public image.

This behavior, management argued, would result in losing customers. The employee had been with the company a long time and had a good work record. The employee sued, but the judge sided with the company.

Generally, courts do not protect employees when their conduct is directly opposed to the company's mission, values or image.

If the off-duty behavior directly impacts work, even though the behavior did not occur at work, termination is usually legal. For instance, an employee who is arrested and spends several weeks in jail may be terminated for absenteeism.

Gray Areas. What about an accountant who gets arrested for child abuse? What if the accountant got arrested for embezzling funds from his church? What if the employee is arrested but not yet convicted? What about a political extremist? Suppose an employee makes "dirty movies" at home?

Why Company Guidelines are Important

To ensure fairness for both employer and employee, it is a good idea to develop policies for off-the-job behavior. Reasonable guidelines include prohibitions against:

- Conduct that represents conflict of interest.
- Use of company equipment.
- Conduct opposed to the company's image and values.
- Wearing company uniforms, logos, and hats when participating in public activities.

It is also helpful when the policy includes the likely consequences for such behaviors. In all cases, use common sense. A supervisor, strongly opposed to abortion, terminated a young single woman who commented that she thought she might have an abortion. Although the employee had a good work record, her supervisor terminated her because, "She did not keep the coffee urns properly filled." The employee sued and won.

Generally, off-duty conduct is none of management's business. But when conduct affects work performance or goes against the clear public image and company mission, it may become grounds for dismissal.

G. A Textbook Approach for Disciplining Problem Employees

To the question, "Does anyone have a problem employee?" I typically receive a resounding, "Yes!" When I ask, "How would you describe your problem employee?" managers report examples such as: "The employee told me that he would decide whether my assignment was a part of his job or not." "She comes to work every day, but she is negative about everything." "He is a good worker when he is here. Unfortunately, he is seldom here." "Not only does she make a lot of mistakes, she is also very slow."

It is easy enough to identify flawed workers. Their actions grab our attention. Many managers lack confidence, it seems, in what to do about their plight.

Consider the Following Checklist When Disciplining Employees

Consider applying these suggestions in sequence. That is, if the first action does not improve the problem, try the next one, and so on.

1. **Counsel and coach**—Tell troublesome employees precisely what they are doing that causes problems. Be honest and specific. Give examples. Avoid general terms like "attitude," "cooperation," "commitment," and the like. Explain exactly what you need from the employee in the future. Coach him on how to do it. Do this two or three times. In my experience, about 15 percent of the "problems" respond to this approach.

2. **Recognize good behavior**—Few employees are 100 percent bad to the bone. Even those who behave like confused adolescents surely have some redeeming features. Look for the positives and brag to the employee about them. Do this very soon after your "counsel and coach" session.

[228]

3. **Verbal reprimand**—Say to the employee, "You know, I've talked with you three times about this. I'm concerned and I'm getting impatient. Consider this a verbal reprimand. If you continue, I'll write you up." Do not, under any circumstances, enter into a catfight with the employee. Your odds of getting a lasting, positive result are about 1 in 4.

4. **Written reprimand**—Write the employee. Follow your company policy. Ask (do not require) the employee to sign the reprimand to confirm only that he/she has seen it. Invite the employee to include his/her notes or rebuttal. You are getting pretty serious now. You will dislodge about 1 in 3 employees from their bad behaviors.

5. **Refer to the Employee Assistance Program**—Suggest (require if you policy allows) that your employee visit with a counselor in your Employee Assistance Program. This suggestion applies only if you have such a program, of course. About half will respond positively.

6. **Terminate**—Calmly, professionally, and firmly (and with support of your Human Resource Management personnel) terminate the employee.

If you do not have the stomach or the ability to terminate the employee, stop after Step 3. From that point forward, simply ignore the problem. People are not perfect. Resign yourself to living with the predicament.

"The problem is too big to ignore," you say? OK, then go on to Steps 4-6. Remember, "Every good leader has good discipline." Be sure that you have secured the support of your boss and coordinate with your Human Relations Department every step of the way.

Chapter 20: Miscellaneous

◆

(Etcetera, etcetera, etcetera.)

We all have bosses. Bosses are human; therefore bosses have flaws. All managers have some employees that are not as productive as they would like them to be. Some unproductive employees may have been there a long time. All departments want more. Weaker departments often shout the loudest. All organizations have policies, but you can't fix most problems with policies. All managers frequently feel like they are in the middle caught between the forces of the leaders and the led. Of some things in life you can be sure: politicians argue and blame, your street will need improving, taxes will increase, and you will experience one or more bad bosses. What to do?

A. How to Deal with Your Boss's Many Flaws

I have worked for more than fifteen bosses in my career. All had flaws. Some had more than others. I've been the boss several times in my career. Many of my staff members thought that my leadership was flawed.

Below are complaints that I heard when talking with front-line supervisors. I have also included some suggestions on how to respond.

Micromanager. "I enjoy my job, but my boss likes to micromanage," exclaimed a supervisor. "I wish he would just let me alone to do my job."

Suggestion: Identify an objective (an outcome) that you know is important to your boss. Include a deadline and a measurement. Say to your boss, "Here is what I'd like to do. Let me work on this project on my own. I'll give you status reports and check with you if I need help. I understand that I will be accountable for achieving the objective."

Information Hoarder. "My boss holds onto information like it was gold. He says he will tell us what we need to know."

Suggestion: In a one-on-one visit, ask the boss if he would be more willing to discuss upcoming changes that impact your employees. Give specific examples of information that you would like to receive so that you can report it to your staff.

Second-guesser. "I have the world's top 'second-guesser.' Whatever decision I make, he will always ask, 'Why didn't you do this? Or why didn't you do that?'"

Suggestion: Say to your boss, "I suppose I could have considered other options. At the time, I thought my decision was based on sound reasoning."

Difference in methods. "My boss wants everything in writing. Every time I begin to make a suggestion, he will say, 'That sounds like a good idea. Why don't you write that up for me?'"

Suggestion: Put your idea in writing.

Takes Credit. "My boss likes to take credit. If something goes wrong though, he is quick to put the blame on someone else."

Suggestion: This boss likes attention. Praise him when you can. Whenever you communicate an achievement, be sure to include the names of people who contributed. Say to your boss, "I know they would feel much appreciated if we gave them a little recognition."

Never Satisfied. "Whatever I do, it is never enough. Last quarter we were almost eight percent ahead of plan. All he could talk about was a couple of opportunities he thought I had missed."

Suggestion: Do not worry about it. You know when you have done a good job.

Deceiver. "My boss misrepresents things. He exaggerates or leaves out things. Sometimes he actually says things that I know are not true."

Suggestion: Make sure you keep good documentation on what you do. If this boss's deception is serious and frequent, when you get specific evidence, consider reporting the incident to an appropriate office, for example, your company hotline or Human Resources.

While I think you should attempt these suggestions, I am fully aware that your boss is not likely to dramatically change. Too many subordinates create too much stress by trying to get the boss to lead in the way that they want to be led. Things might go easier for you if you first try to find out how your boss wants things done and accommodate him.

Do not expect your boss to be perfect. No human is. A forgotten wit once proclaimed, "I may not always be right, but I am always the boss."

B. How to Manage a Long-Time, Non-Productive Employee

"Here's my problem," began a flustered manager. "Marie works in my department. She makes mistakes. She tries to intimidate younger workers, and she negatively impacts other departments."

"How long has she been with the company?"

"She is sixty-two years old and has been with the company thirty-five years. I inherited her when I became the manager three years ago."

"Has she recently had an opportunity to go through training?"

"Yes, she went through a complete training program along with ten others in the department just last year. She complained a lot about having to do it."

"Have you tried coaching her yourself?"

"Yes, I've taken time to talk with her and suggested several things to do differently. She argues, and may go along with the suggestions for awhile. Soon she reverts to her non-productive behaviors."

"Is there anything else?"

"Yes, she bullies other employees, tells them how to do their jobs, and complains loudly when asked to do something that she does not want to do. Sometimes she flatly refuses."

"Have you talked with your Human Resources Director about her?"

"Yes. He said, 'She has been with the company a long time. Try to work with her if you can. If you think that you need to recommend termination, you will need a lot of documentation.'"

Options for Dealing with Long-Time, Non-productive Employees

The long-time, non-productive employee presents managers a between a rock-and-a-hard place challenge. Here are your alternatives.

1. **Accept the situation.** One option is to accept the situation. Just put up with it. Other employees may whine and moan. You may have to spend time cleaning up after the employee. The employee is not going to change.

Is this the right choice for you? Ask yourself the question: "Is it right for the company, our customers, and other employees to allow this employee to continue his/her current behavior?" I expect the answer is a resounding, "No." If so, consider Option 2.

2. **Apply damage control.** Option 2 is to severely reduce the employee's responsibilities. Very narrowly define what the employee will do. Strip off as many assignments as possible. Assign any meaningful work to others. Pay no attention to the whining that is sure to occur. You are not trying to purposefully make the employee unhappy. You are simply trying to lessen the employee's impact on others.

3. **Performance Improvement Plan.** Put the employee on a Performance Improvement Plan (PIP). Work with your Human Resources Department to identify specific performance improvements that the employee needs to make. Use performance data to communicate your dissatisfaction with current performance.

   Identify specific improvement targets that the employee must make. Designate a reasonable and specific date for achieving improvement targets. Explain that the improvements must be permanent. In some cases, employees will hit the improvement goals for awhile and then swerve back to previous unacceptable levels.

4. **Document and terminate.** Should the employee not maintain satisfactory performance levels, you have the documentation for termination. If your company has an early retirement program, consider it if the employee is eligible.

   If "document and terminate" is the right option, this should not cause undue guilt or anxiety for the manager. Long-term employment does not earn employees the right to strictly serve their own personal interests. Nor does it earn them the right to be destructive and distracting to other employees who are working hard to serve the company mission.

C. If You Allocate Resources to Marginal Producers, You Will Ensure Mediocrity

Meetings over budget allocations often resemble combat zones. Everyone fights for more of whatever it is that is being allocated. We perform well. We deserve more. We perform poorly, we need more.

Consider the excerpts below. Two department heads are making persuasive presentations in their budget meetings.

"I need more resources for Accounts Receivables. We are having a lot of trouble meeting our collection objectives."

"If you will give me a half dozen more people in the Consulting Department, we can increase revenues even more rapidly than we did last year."

What to do? Shore up the weak link? Or, water where the flowers grow?

Managers usually allocate internal resources along the following lines.

Everyone Gets Something

We are all on the same team. We have to take care of everyone. None of us may get as much as we want. We will all get something. All groups get about the same percentage increase or decrease in their budgets for next year.

This method of spreading the resources around may help forestall palace revolts. Most managers take what they get. Some will grumble a bit. Few will muster the energy to declare war against their leadership.

But a more-or-less equal division of the spoils does not encourage excellence. It ensures mediocrity. Such a strategy encourages the belief, "It doesn't matter what you accomplish. Everyone gets the same thing."

Great performers may not revolt, but they may migrate to more effective organizations.

Problems with High to Low Allocations

Allocate more to substandard performers. A chain is only as strong as its weakest link. High performing departments are doing fine. We have to shore up our weaknesses.

Although more common than you might think, this strategy, in my view, at best supports inefficiency. At its worst the result is disaster. Low contributing departments do not turn into "Cinderella's" simply because they receive a little more budget or headcount.

You are just throwing good money after bad. Neither low performing groups nor low performing individuals perform better or faster or more efficiently simply by getting a little more resource.

If a department, division, or employee consistently delivers second-rate results, make drastic changes. Outsource the function. If this is not feasible, consider major surgery such as replacing people.

Do not try to cure low performances by drawing down from effective groups and allocating to the less effective.

Invest in the Best

You have done well. There is probably even more opportunity there. We will allocate more to you. Your outstanding performance earned more resources.

I observed a franchise with 45 stores. A new owner invested budget and personnel to improve the performance of all stores. By the end of the year, the top 10 stores improved profitability by 20 percent. The worst stores improved only 2 percent. The next year, the owner closed some of the poor stores and sold the others.

Intuitively, we think that there is more room for improvement among low performing functions or employees, but facts do not support this judgment.

Rather, research clearly demonstrates that people or departments who are already performing well actually have more upside improvements than departments or individuals with disappointing results.

Organizations achieve excellence by improving their strengths. As researchers Buckingham and Coffman say in their book, *First Break All the Rules*, "Invest in the best. It is the only avenue to excellence."

D. No Matter How Well Designed, Policies Do Not Cure Problems

Do you tend to "agree" or "disagree" with the following:

1. Policies have a strong influence on employee behavior.
2. Most employees have good attendance because of attendance policies.
3. Policies prohibiting employee theft are very effective.
4. Performance review policies result in effective appraisals.
5. Sick leave policies drastically reduce employee abuse of sick leave.

The correct answer to all of the above, according to my experience, is "disagree."

Shortly after Gordon Bethune took over as president of Continental Airlines, he publicly burned their very thick company manual.

According to Bethune, "…we had rules—specific rules—for everything from what color pencil had to be used on boarding passes to what kind of meals delayed passengers were supposed to be given to what kind of fold ought to be put in a sick-day form."

Even with all of these specific policies, rules and regulations, Continental was dead last in practically every industry performance measure.

Problems with Policies

Some policies are general and some are specific. All policies try to tell managers how to prevent, cure or otherwise fix problems. But there are no defined and reliable steps for creating happy customers.

Work conditions change rapidly and often. Policies have the life of oak trees. Most all organizations have outdated written policies.

Policies provide "cover." Employees can escape accountability for results by documenting the fact that they followed the policy.

"Make sure you follow all of the safety policies," exhorted a manager. "If we have an accident, we want to make sure we're covered."

Policies discourage initiative and trust. Employees soon learn to just follow the policies.

Are There Any Benefits?

If policies create so many problems, why then do all companies insist on having policies? In short, two reasons.

One, policies allow managers to discipline non-productive employees.

Companies that have attendance policies still have attendance problems. But the policy allows the manager to terminate employees who have awful attendance.

Performance appraisal policies do not increase employee output. But appraisals allow managers to grant low or zero pay increases to low performers.

Two, policies give companies legal cover.

Safety policies do not eliminate all accidents. They may allow companies strong legal defenses against careless employees.

Policies against falsifying records and cheating do not prevent the acts.

Such policies do allow companies to legally punish employees who lie and cheat.

Do I suggest burning your policy manual? No. (Bethune appointed a task force and created a new less restrictive manual.)

I do suggest that you not operate under the delusion that policies will cure your problems. It takes good leadership, good training and good staff to do that.

E. You Must Learn to Lead from the Middle

Barbara's boss had just given her a tight deadline for completing a complex project. Barbara manages a staff of twenty-four.

When told of the deadline, one staff member said, "With our current resources, the deadline is unrealistic."

Another chimed in, "I don't see how upper management can expect us to meet the deadline unless they allocate more headcount to our group."

Three others, good friends with the two, agreed.

Over the next couple of weeks, two of the "five" put too much time on lesser priorities. A third member requested vacation time. Another used some "family emergency" leave.

Barbara's department lost headcount during the previous year. Although volume has increased, upper management has not allocated new resources.

To her most recent request, Barbara's boss responded. "Barbara, competition has increased. I do not see significant additions to your budget in the near future."

Barbara also knows that to have a chance for a successful project, she will need the full commitment of all of her staff.

"I feel like I'm in the middle," explained Barbara. "I support our mission. I understand what corporate wants. I understand why. A few staff members are outright obstacles. Many feel threatened. Morale is low."

Advocate for Staff?

It is tempting for leaders in Barbara's position to advocate for staff.

For instance, the group of five suggested, "Give upper management two choices. One, to meet current deadlines, we will need four additional staff members. Two, with no additional resources, we will need a three-month extension."

This is a "no win" position.

The odds of getting additional resources are very low. Staff members will feel like their leader has failed them. More importantly, the project will not be completed on time.

Manipulate Staff?

Some leaders attempt to manipulate staff.

Barbara could meet privately with the resistors. Ask for their commitment. In return, she could make future promises—good reviews, pay increases, choice job assignments, and support for their favorite projects.

This is another "no win."

Suppose the resistors step up and complete the project on time. Their expectations of a pay off from Barbara will likely far exceed anything that she could realistically deliver. If they do not complete the project, they will still want to collect on Barbara's promises.

Lead Staff?

During crunch time, a leader's role is to deliver, even when staff members believe that they should not or cannot do the job.

I suggest the following. Without equivocating, explain the deadline. Listen empathetically to doubts, but hold firm. Without arguing, use logic to persuade the group why the deadline is important. Lay out a plan of how the deadline can be met.

After the meeting, Barbara should visit one-on-one with each of the dissenters and ask for their help. If they resist, Barbara should clearly explain that she expects them to treat the project as their highest priority.

Provide regular status updates. Passionately praise all successes. When segments get behind, request input from staff, offer plans for catching up, reassign people if necessary, but always stress the necessity of making the deadline.

Managers often feel like they are caught in the middle, because they are. However, managers are part of the leadership team. So long as upper management's requests are legal, ethical and moral, managers should put corporate mission above individual distracters.

F. When Saddled with a Bad Boss, Perform — Don't Complain

"My boss is a jerk! That's the only way you can describe him."

"What does he do that is so bad?"

"He distorts things. He told me the vice president disapproved of my proposal. I found out that he was the one who didn't like it."

"Is that all?"

"No, he grabs credit for things he did not do. He doesn't tell us things. When he is around us, he criticizes top management. When he is with them, he blames us for things that were his fault, kiss up and kick down; I think that is what they call it."

"I'll bet there is more."

"Oh yes, he thinks he never makes a mistake. It's always someone else's fault and..."

"What are you going to do about it?"

Jack Welch, former leader of General Electric and author of the book, *Winning*, offers suggestions for dealing with a bad boss.

Do Not be a Victim

No matter how much your boss makes you want to whine and moan, don't do it. You feel like complaining endlessly at the water fountain; bite your tongue. You want to unload on supportive colleagues; resist the urge. You feel like creating an insurrection to attack the castle, think again.

If you get so frustrated you are about to bust, take your dog for a walk and vent to the dog. Your dog will understand and you will feel better.

This is your problem. You will have to accept it, deal with it or end it. But keep up a good attitude while you are deciding what to do.

Can You Still Produce Good Results?

If you can produce great results in spite of your boss, do so. Spend more time with subordinates. Get out in the field. Visit with customers. Associate with good performers. Kick your performance up a notch.

Producing good work is the best way to gain creditability with others. Other managers may even help you without you knowing it.

Don't get your hopes up. Your boss is not going to change even if you deliver record-setting performance. Jerks develop at early ages and usually remain so throughout their careers. Still you can get satisfaction and personal fulfillment by knowing that you have produced eye-popping numbers.

Avoid End Runs

While it may sometimes help, understand that it is risky to rat out your boss to his superiors. More likely your sincere efforts only come back to bite you.

If the superior agrees with your assessment and admonishes your boss, chances are your boss will figure out that you were involved. Remember, he is a jerk. Do not expect him to react maturely to the criticism.

Look at the Big Picture

Do you like what you do? Do you like your colleagues? Do you and your family like living in the area? Do you think you can continue to grow professionally and personally? Are your earnings competitive?

Life, and your job, is full of trade-offs. If the benefits outweigh the negatives, you are probably ahead.

If your frustration is record-setting high, if there is no potential long-term relief, then prepare your job search plan and get out with as little damage as possible.

Understand the boss is not going to change. It is your choice to go or stay. Should you choose to stay, come to grips with the fact you are staying by choice. Should you decide to go, do not look back. Either way, you are not a victim; make the choice that is right for you.